A Shaking Reality

A Shaking Reality

Daily Reflections for Advent

Peter B. Price

DARTON·LONGMAN+TODD

First published in 2018 by
Darton, Longman and Todd Ltd
1 Spencer Court
140 – 142 Wandsworth High Street
London SW18 4JJ

ISBN: 978-0-232-53350-7

A catalogue record for this book is available from the British Library

Phototypeset by Kerrypress, St Albans AL3 8JL
Printed and bound in Great Britain by Bell & Bain, Glasgow

For Chris,
friend, mentor,
and Advent guide

Contents

Introduction

'Walking up and down my cell three paces this way, three paces that way, with my hands in irons and ahead of me an uncertain future, I have a new and different understanding of God's promise of redemption and release.'

These words were written by Father Alfred Delp during Advent 1944 from his cell in Plotonzee Prison in Nazi Germany. Delp belonged to a small group of courageous men and women who committed themselves to building a new Christian order after the war. Alfred had been imprisoned for 'defeatism' and treason. He was hanged in prison on 2 February 1945, the Feast of the Presentation of Christ in the Temple.

In that place of an 'uncertain future' and with his 'hands in irons', Delp penned a meditation entitled *The Shaking Reality of Advent*. He described Advent as 'a time when we all ought to be shaken and brought to a realisation of ourselves'. He saw it as providing an opportunity for bringing people to their senses, to live, work and pray for God to intervene in human affairs in order to bring in a new world order of justice, love and peace.

Some years ago, my friend and mentor Christine Roberts introduced me to Delp's testimony. The courage and witness of his story, and of others like him, have provided inspiration for these Advent reflections. Here are people of faith who have been 'shaken' and 'brought to a realisation of themselves'. In so doing, they have provided a testimony that invites us to gain 'a new understanding of God's promise of redemption and release'.

Throughout the history of peoples of faith there has been an expectation of a God who will intervene in human affairs and bring peace. The prophet Isaiah describes the 'One who comes' as - 'Messiah', 'Wonderful Counsellor, Mighty God, Prince of Peace'[1] and a 'suffering Servant'.[2] Christians identify Jesus Christ, born in Bethlehem, as the One who in God's Name bears all such expectation. But such a claim is not without controversy or contradiction.

The Jewish philosopher and teacher, Martin Buber, addressing a conference of Jews and Christians in the aftermath of the *Shoah*, the Nazi holocaust in Europe, said: 'You Christians say that the Messiah has already come, whilst we Jews await his coming. I suggest that when he comes, we ask him, "Were you here before?" And I hope', he paused, 'I hope to be near enough to whisper in his ear, "For the love of heaven, don't answer".'[3]

It is a poignant story. The Nazi pogroms led to the largest systematic murder of Jews ever witnessed. Such a happening emerged from a continent whose rulers defined Christendom. It was a horror that the German theologian, Dorothee Söelle, described as filling her with an 'ineradicable shame'. We should not be surprised, given the experience of his people, that Buber expressed the desire to avoid controversy.

Advent is a time for penitence, as well as a time of hope. In Christendom, when emperors and monarchs perceived themselves as Christians, and by definition their peoples were Christian too,

---

1   Isaiah 9:5 –7

2   Isaiah 52:13 – 53:12

3   The story is adapted from that told by Elie Wiesel in *All Rivers Run to the Sea* (Knopf, 1995)

state and Church were inextricably bound together. No longer was Jesus the beaten, reviled crucified Christ, the victim of an unholy alliance of religion and politics. Now Christ had become the one who ruled through power and prestige, whose patronage his emissaries could claim as 'God and my right'.

Those days are past. Christendom has come to an end. Christianity itself is experiencing a time of 'shaking'. And if not yet a time of 'self realisation', then certainly a time of questioning. A time to ask just who is the Christ that Advent bids us welcome? A time to consider where is God's reign of justice, love and peace? Where are his people committed to compassion, mercy, love and truth?

The season of Advent offers to us the possibility of 'a new understanding of God's promise of redemption and release'. In the busyness of Christmas preparations, Advent craves space to reflect upon what it means to welcome the 'coming' Christ into our lives, our world, our future. Advent bids us look towards a God, who in the words of Dorothee Söelle,[4] 'does not float above history and its trauma, but shares intimately in the suffering of the victims.'

In Advent we seek God's presence from the space we occupy. Unlike Alfred Delp, few if any readers of this book will be 'walking up and down a cell three paces this way, three paces that way with hands in irons'. Chains may not bind us, but we are constrained by the place, circumstances and time in which we live. We sense our hands are tied by self-limitation, relationships, work, and the expectation of others.

---

4   Dorothee Söelle was fifteen years old when the Second World War ended in her native Germany. For the remainder of her life she sought to challenge and understand how Christians had employed the excuse that 'they did not know about plans and preparations for mass murder'.

Often, too, as we look at the world around us, we feel that our hands are tied and there is nothing we can do about its suffering and injustice.

Advent invites us to find time and space to discern afresh the God who comes among us. The story is told of a housekeeper to a very busy priest. One day she took a peek into his diary to see just what occupied him so fully, but why he seemed so serene. To her surprise the only entries to the diary were four words written at the head of each page: 'Breathe in, breathe out'. The reflections in this book have been designed to be long enough for the reader to find a rhythm for solitude - to 'breathe in, and breathe out' - but short enough to fit into the busyness of life.

A devout African-American woman living in the Southern States of America, who had known hardship all her life, called her pastor to visit her. 'When I die, pastor,' she requested, 'I want you to place a dessert fork in my left hand when I lie in my open coffin and people come to see me.' 'Why a dessert fork?' queried the puzzled pastor. 'Because', replied the woman, 'when I was a child and we were very poor, we rarely had dessert. But when there was a dessert fork set at the table, I knew there was something better to come. That is how I want people to see my death. It is in the hope of something better to come.'

Advent challenges us to face the realities of our world. To see the violence, observe the suffering, feel the hardship, and, in whatever ways we can, seek the God who 'does not float above history and its trauma, but shares intimately in the suffering of the victims' and invites us to do the same.

Advent holds the promise of 'something better to come'. A time for 'waking out of sleep'. A time of refusing to despair. A time for changing our ways. A time to free God to re-enter and re-make this world. A time to acknowledge that we are not the

4

only people of faith who have expectation in looking for the 'One who is to come'.

Christmas is an ambiguous time. It neither marks in historical time the date of the birth of Christ, nor is it based on a 'Christian' festival that has been corrupted by time. It is rather the other way round. In the cold, northern climes, around the shortest day of the year, people celebrated the end of darkness and the beginning of light. It had many names, of which the best known is 'The Birthday of the un-conquered sun' - in Latin *Dies Natalia solis invicti*.

It was on this event that emergent Christianity hung its celebration of Christ our Light. Advent challenges us, not to try to change the party that people want to have in the mid-winter, but rather to re-engage ourselves with an understanding of what the birth of Christ means to us, who call ourselves the 'People of God'. If, for us, 'Jesus is the reason for the season', then in a post- Christian Era, the challenge that exists for us is to understand more fully how to participate in making known Jesus' work in restoring all humanity to participate in God's justice and goodness.

Advent invites us not to judge others, which is expressly forbidden by Jesus, but rather to allow ourselves to come under God's gracious and restoring judgment. It is a season of *resistance*. A time to turn with greater urgency to worship, prayer and dedication to resist all that seeks to destroy abundant living, and prevents God's purposes from being fulfilled.

Advent is a time of *reclamation*. A time to reclaim the truth of the message of the angels: 'Peace on earth' through the practice of non-violence, love, compassionate justice, true repentance and forgiveness. It is a time to reclaim a counter-narrative to the world's agenda of 'peace and security' through 'military solutions' and 'wars against terror'. A time to follow the child of Bethlehem by being sensitive and responsive to suffering and injustice.

Advent too, is a time for *re-membrance*. A time to draw the whole past into the present. To enter Bethlehem, to see the Child, 'God from God, Light from Light'. A time to be caught up in the love of the God we cannot see. A time to wonder at the simplicity and profundity of the infant Christ, who contains the full presence of the Living God. A time to *re-member* 'this is the truth sent from above, the truth of God, the God of love', as the ancient carol has it; and in penitence to respond to its plea: 'therefore don't turn me from your door, but hearken all, both rich and poor.' *Re-membrance* is the key to the future; only through the recovery of *memory* can 'Peace on earth' be achieved.

As Alfred Delp discovered in his prison cell, Advent is a time of '*redemption* and release'. 'The word *redemption* means to reacquire or reestablish the covenant of God with his people as promised by the prophets.'[5] On Christmas night, we are drawn to the table of the Lord to participate in drinking from the 'cup of the new covenant'.[6] We hear the words: 'This is my body which is given for you … This is my blood which is shed for you. Do this in *remembrance* of me.' Then we eat, and drink. We do so to re-enter the covenant, to re-make the promise that we will share in Christ's sacrifice, his death and resurrection: here and now.

Advent then calls us to risk being 'shaken and brought to a realisation of ourselves'. To discover afresh the truth that 'the horror of these times would be unendurable, unless we kept being cheered and set up right by the promises that are spoken'. To trust

---

5   Joseph Grassi, *Peace on Earth: Roots and Practices from Luke's Gospel* (Liturgical Press, p.142)

6   Luke 22:20

again the God-inspired promises announced by prophets, saints and angels relayed in Readings, Prayers and Carols.

Each person who reads this book will do so from a different place. Some will have a sense of being constrained 'three paces this way, three paces that way with hands in irons'. Others will read it from a 'wide open space' - as the Hebrew word for salvation has it. My prayer is that from whatever space you now occupy you will be led into a 'new and different understanding of God's promise of redemption and release'.

Getting Ready

As the leaves of Autumn start to turn, my preparation for Advent begins. I scour book reviews and talk with friends about what to read. I look for liturgies that might give me a fresh perspective on God's promise of redemption and release. The resources gathered, like a squirrel hoarding food I hide them away until Advent dawns.

For more than fifty years we have made an Advent wreath from greenery collected from hedgerows and woods. Five new candles - three purple, marking the patriarchs and matriarchs, the prophets and John the Baptist; one pink for Mary the Mother of God; and one white for the birth of the Christ Child - are added. All are placed on a stand. The candles will be lit on each of the four Sundays, and then on Christmas Day itself.

When our children were growing up, we set the Advent wreath in the entrance to our house. Each night candles were lit. An Advent Calendar adorned the wall. Behind each day's 'doorway' some picture of the Christmas story would appear along with a biblical text. Taking turns each evening one of us would light the candle, open the window, and read the text. Together we prayed an Advent prayer.

'We teach our children how to measure, how to weigh,' observed Rabbi Joshua Herschel. 'We fail to teach them how to revere, how to sense wonder and care.' Often during our Advent observation, a serendipitous moment of stillness settled upon us. A quiet wondering.

Now with just the two of us at home, the wreath is smaller, simpler: the calendar has been replaced with a pyramid of little boxes. Each contains a small surprise and a prayer. We still light the candle and say the prayer. 'Thirty-seven seconds, well used, is a lifetime,' as Mr Magorium observes.[1] Now as we recall more Advents past than to come, we remember, we wait, and we anticipate.

In each of the homes in which we have lived we have sought to create 'sacred space'. Often this has been a simple table in a corner, covered with a cloth, bearing a candle, an icon, a cross and Bible.

For a privileged while we lived in a medieval house where I had a beautiful study. It was a place that came into its own in the winter. I would come downstairs early to light a wood fire in the large grate. Stepping out into the woodshed, I would collect a box of prepared sticks and logs. My first prayer of the day was one of gratitude for friends who had cut, stacked and boxed the wood that would warm my visitors and me each day.

Kneeling at the hearth, striking a match, there was the moment of anticipation as the paper and twigs caught fire. The sight of the first bluey-grey smoke, the crackle of wood, the explosive pum-pum-pum of the flames, followed by the slower, deeper burning of the logs. Later their sweet incense would fill the room, warmed by the gentle heat of glowing embers.

The fire lit. The space prepared. The sounds of crackling wood, and my own breathing in and out, gave way to a gathered stillness. In the window a lamp reflected. Outside a winter moon set beneath the Morning Star. Time to be, not to do. Stillness and the mystery of silence.

---

1   Mr Edward Magorium, played by Dustin Hoffman, in the magical film *Mr Magorium's Wonder Emporium* (2007).

Whilst it is an increasingly distant yet treasured memory, I recall the experience, and appreciate the truth of words from the poet Vera Newsom:

> Young we love, grasp, consume. Old we savour
> And the taste sends us wild.

Today we still create space - especially at Advent. In the tiny hut we grandly call 'The Garden House' hangs a plaque inscribed: '*Bidden or Not, God is present.*' In the delightful story of *The Little Prince,* Antoine de Saint-Exupéry writes of a little boy who comes to Earth from a tiny planet in space. Here he encounters a fox whom he wants to befriend. The shy fox suggests, 'Let us sit near each other and look at one another each day.' By so doing, Prince and fox can gain a fresh perspective. Then, says the fox, 'each day we can move a little closer. Then we can become friends.'

It is a story that serves us well at the beginning of Advent. Advent is a time to both recall and anticipate. We reflect on the familiarity of the nativity story - the One who *has* come. The New Testament offers us two further perspectives: the 'One who *is* come' - present continuous: and the 'One who *will* come' - future.

When Jesus took his leave from his disciples following the resurrection, he promised: '… remember I am with you always to the end of the age.'[2] Here the crucified, risen and soon-to-be ascended One promised a continuous '*is*-ness': 'I shall pour out my Spirit on all humanity.'[3]

St Luke, the author of the Acts of the Apostles, tells us of the 'One who *will* come'. He speaks of 'the coming of the Lord's great

---

2   Matthew 28:20

3   Acts 2:17 (NJB)

and glorious day'.[4] Here, there is a sense of finality, a wrapping up of history. The Book of Revelation puts it poetically: 'See the home of God is among mortals. He will dwell with them; they will be his peoples and God himself will be with them; he will wipe away every tear from their eyes. Death will be no more: mourning and crying will be no more, for the first things have passed away.'[5]

Each day in Advent, like the Little Prince, we are invited to move a little closer to the One who *has, is* and *will* come. Each day provides an opportunity to change our perspective. Each day we can risk re-making friendship with the One who calls us friends. Each day we can face the reality of an 'uncertain future'. And each day we can anticipate 'something better to come'.

Advent can begin on any date from 27 November to the 3 December. This book calculates the first Sunday as being 27 November. To read all the reflections, ending on Christmas Day, whether Advent Sunday falls on that date or not, you might wish to begin your reflection on 27 November.

Each of us is different with differing pressures. Whilst these reflections are designed to be read each day, there is nothing to prevent the reader from reading more than one at a time.

Advent bids us set aside time for reflection. A time to allow for a 'new understanding of God's promise of redemption and release'. A time to respond to whatever Inner Voice speaks from the day's reading. A time to experience Advent's 'shaking reality'. Light a candle. Say the prayer, and let the Ever-Present Presence of the Divine be revealed. 'Breathe in, breathe out.' Learn to 'sit near' and each day move a little closer to the God who *has* come, *is* come, and *will* come again.

---

4   Acts 2:20.

5   Revelation 21:3-4

A Prayer

Almighty God
give us grace to cast away the works of darkness
and put on the armour of light,
now in the time of this mortal life,
in which your Son Jesus Christ came to visit us in great
  humility,
that in the last day
when he shall come again in his glorious majesty
to judge both the quick and the dead,
we may rise to the life immortal;
through him who is alive and reigns with you,
in the unity of the Holy Spirit,
one God, now and for ever.

Collect for the First Sunday in Advent,
Common Worship - Services and Prayers
for the Church of England

The First Sunday
The Abraham Path

Advent begins by looking back in the biblical story of faith to Abraham. He was a man who was shaken up by God. Called to leave his traditional homeland, his securities and his wealth, Abraham entered a new space, becoming the founder of many nations. He became the progenitor of Judaism, Christianity and Islam, all three faiths acknowledging him as their source.

Some years ago William Ury, a Harvard professor, had a vision to construct an 'Abraham Path'. This was to be a trail designed to link all the places associated with the life of Abraham. Beginning in Harran in Turkey, where Abraham heard God's call to 'Go from your country',[1] the path is projected to pass through Syria, Turkey, Jordan, Israel, Palestine and Egypt. It is his hope that by travelling the trail, people will come to see a different face of the Middle East. Here they would discover that people here are not different, but fellow humans like ourselves, all part of a greater whole.

Unwittingly I have walked sections of the 'Abraham Path', unaware of its significance and intent. I have dined in the Wadi Kelt on the edge of the desert, received hospitality from Bedouin people, and shared in the company of Jews and Muslims striving to live together. During these simple, moving occasions, I have

---

1   Genesis 12:1 – 4

15

listened to stories, shared experiences, and celebrated the essential 'one-ness' of our common humanity.

At other times I have crossed and re-crossed the border between Israel and the Occupied Territories. Standing in the dawn line amongst Palestinian workers, I have witnessed the daily de-humanisation of one people by another. I have seen on both sides how 'hurt people, hurt people', as the mystic Simone Weil put it. In the Beit Sahour district of Bethlehem I have watched and listened to Palestinians and Israelis seeking healing and reconciliation.

Ury recognised that the conflicts of the Middle East affect all of us, Christian, Muslim and Jew: this is all our story. The 'Abraham Path' crosses some ten countries of nations armed to the teeth, carrying a history of suspicion, fear and conflict. When, 4000 years ago, Abraham left the security of his homeland and travelled across tribal lands, he did so as an act of unity, and kindness towards strangers.

Envisioning the 'Abraham Path', Ury foresaw the possibility of people walking together. By walking side by side, shoulder to shoulder, people have to listen to, and touch each other. It was a vision of the long haul. People who walk together, side by side, cannot fight.

Conflict, violence and mass migration impede the completion of the Path. These realities symbolise the ongoing division and distrust among those who claim Abraham as their 'father'.

Change is slow. Building the 'Abraham Path' is a Herculean task. In mythology, Hercules, as an act of penance for killing his family, accepted the discipline of performing twelve apparently impossible tasks to appease the gods. Ury's vision in some sense is an act of atonement for the destructiveness and division between Jew, Christian and Muslim.

Completing the 'Path' remains difficult. Stubbornness and ongoing conflicts limit negotiations. Yet, whilst still incomplete, the 'Path' is already more than a line on the map. Though the task of fully establishing it remains a long-term goal, the dream will now be difficult to erase. Many people have been inspired by the idea of the 'Abraham Path', but they know they will have little likelihood of ever travelling it. So they have created their own. At significant festivals groups of folks have marked them by making a pilgrimage walk from church, to mosque and synagogue. Together in Abrahamic unity, they have shared stories, experiences and each other's hospitality.

The Old Testament describes Abraham as 'friend of God'. Abraham perceived the truth that 'God is One'. It is a truth that forms the basis of Judaism, Christianity and Islam. The Book of Genesis depicts God as seeking relationship with Abraham, entrusting him to pass on the truth of 'God is One' to future generations. As a consequence, God and Abraham covenant, or agree, to bind together all humanity, so that it may enjoy the fulness of life.[2]

During Advent we light candles each Sunday. Today the 'Candle of Hope' is lit. It reminds us that long before Jesus was born, his ancestors hoped that one day earth's Redeemer would come and fulfil God's purposes for humanity. We too are invited to walk the 'Abraham Path', befriending the stranger, sharing simple hospitality and promoting unity.

Alfred Delp in his prison cell understood that Advent's 'shaking reality' begins with the realisation of the need for 'a new and different understanding of God's promise of redemption and release'. As we look for the 'Coming One', whose birth in

---

2   Genesis 15

Bethlehem we now prepare to celebrate, we are reminded that to achieve such unity, Jesus was to lay down his life to inaugurate the 'great nation' of truth, beauty and love.

A prayer

Lord God,
you have given us a dwelling place
and a city to build up,
people to live with.
Open our eyes, make us
solicitous for one another,
for those who have no hope, or future.
Make us small enough
to go with them and serve them,
then we shall build each other up
for a new future,
where God will be justice and peace.

Prayer in Bruges Cathedral

The First Monday
Hurt people hurt people

One of the great sadnesses in life is when a couple want a child and are unable to conceive. It hurts. Painful and difficult questions are raised. Is there something wrong with either of us? What if it is me? Irrational questions too. Has something happened in the past that has brought this pain and suffering? In darkest moments, people even question whether in some way it is something that they have 'deserved' because of some long-forgotten wrong-doing.

Sometimes the pain is so great, and the questions so unanswerable, that separation and divorce follow. The happiness of others for whom a loved and longed-for child, or children, appear to have come so easily, leaves a deep chasm of bereavement for those not so blessed.

Abraham had been given a promise to be the progenitor of many nations. However, Sarah and he were unable to conceive that promised 'first-born' who would set in train the 'great nation', numerous as 'stars in the night sky'.[1] How is Abraham to 'father' a people? Can God be trusted for Sarah to become the 'mother'? What does their infertility mean? Is there another way?

We may reasonably presume that such questions formed in their minds and hearts. One solution did present itself. Sarah had a slave named Hagar. In the culture of the times, slave women

---

1   Genesis 15:4

often slept with the tribal chief. Sarah offers this to Abraham as a solution. Could an heir be conceived through a surrogate, Hagar?[2] Even to God-fearing Abraham, Hagar as a slave would have been treated as 'property'.

How much choice Hagar had in the plan is questionable. In due course she fell pregnant. Sarah immediately regretted her decision, and treated Hagar so badly that the slave woman tried to run away. Following a vision from God, Hagar chose to stay and put up with her lot. It would be easy at this point to take this story at face value. But here's the thing: the 'shaking reality' is not only that Hagar was to be the mother of the first-born, but that in a patriarchal age God spoke and made promises to a *woman,* and somebody's property at that.

In matters of faith and trust, obedience is all. Abraham and Sarah's impatience, and apparent disbelief, is confounded. Miracle of miracles, Sarah becomes pregnant. God is faithful. Now an opportunity exists for a moment of grace. But too often 'hurt people hurt people'. Despite the fulfilment of God's promise, Sarah demands that Abraham banish Hagar and Ishmael, the son she conceived with Abraham, to the desert. It was effectively the passing of a sentence of death.

Abraham's brutal callousness was a direct consequence of a refusal to trust God's promise. Everything else followed. Sarah feared that Isaac, son of the Promise, and Ishmael, the son of practicality, would grow up as equals. Such equality would be culturally unacceptable. Abraham, 'friend of God' though he might be, could not face such a prospect. The only solution to his dilemma, Abraham concluded, was for Hagar and Ishmael to die in the desert.

---

2   Genesis 16

Once again Abraham reckons without God. God refuses to abandon Hagar and Ishmael (whose name means 'God hears'), but God rescues them.[3] Hagar glimpses the 'shaking reality' of God's wider purpose. She names - *el roi* - 'the God who sees'. Outsider, woman of no account she may be to others; but to God who 'hears' and 'sees', Hagar is of equal value and worth. Like Abraham, she too receives a promise, that her son will lead a great nation. He will be the progenitor of the Arab people.

This is a story that comforts and discomforts. It reveals that God 'hears' the cries of the oppressed, and 'sees' their distress, and blesses them with hope. The 'shaking reality' of this story is that it exposes those who consider themselves God's favourites as sinful and arrogant. It reveals the shocking truth that God has no favourites; all who are born, whether out of practicality or promise, share equal status in God's eyes. Abraham's friendship with God did not make him special, but an emissary of God's desire for humanity to be united, and to share together at a common table. Not only is God 'One', but humanity made in God's image is to be one too.

A Prayer

Loving God, you long for us to live in peace,
we grieve with you for the violence in our world.
Help us to protect the vulnerable and all who suffer,
offering with love a safe place for all in need.

A Prayer from the United
Society of Partners in Mission

---

3   Genesis 21

The First Tuesday
Put to the test

A female colleague and I stood beside the barrier in Gaza city that divides the Occupied Territories from Israel - a blockage on the 'Abraham Path'. It was International Women's Day and earlier we had each been given a rose, one red, one white. Spontaneously we stepped up to the barrier and placed the roses in small cracks. We bowed our heads and offered silent prayer for peace, an end to bloodshed and all that divides humanity.

As we stepped away from the barrier the story of Hagar and Sarah took on a contemporary reality. Sarah represented women who had status and privilege, powerful and able to take initiatives. Her influence over Abraham and her ruthless treatment of Hagar evidenced this. Such was her arrogance that when promised a child she laughed at God in disbelief.[1]

Hagar represented women without freedom, subject to the whims of others, victims of their cruelty and brutality. Yet people like Hagar so often find hope in God in a way that those who are more materially secure and powerful do not.

Hagar shared with Abraham the experience of being directly addressed by God. Hagar intuitively knew that only God could save her, and fulfil the promise of her son Ishmael becoming the

---

1 Genesis 18:12

founder of a great nation.[2] But Abraham had to learn how God saves, because he had refused to trust God to fulfil his promise.

During their banishment in the desert, Hagar and Ishmael faced the real possibility of dying. Knowing of the desert's harsh ways, Abraham had callously calculated this is as a way of saving Isaac, the son of the Promise. Hagar and Ishmael could be written off as collateral damage on the path to achieving God's purpose.

Once again, Abraham reckoned without God. God, having witnessed Abraham's willingness to allow Hagar and Ishmael to die for the sake of the Promise, now tests Abraham. God challenges Abraham to sacrifice Isaac.[3] It is a shocking suggestion. The Jewish writer Elie Wiesel has pointed out that Jewish tradition does not permit death to be used as a means of glorifying God; and no human being has a right to sacrifice another, not even to God.[4]

Abraham acquiesces, even though he knows what God is demanding is wrong. At the site of sacrifice, Isaac questions who or what is to be sacrificed. 'God will provide' declares Abraham. Bound and tied to the funeral pyre, Abraham lifts the knife. Is there to be a last-minute stay of execution? Will Abraham go through with it? Elie Wiesel suggests that as Abraham lifted the knife, he did so saying to God: 'I defy you Lord. I shall submit to your will but let us see whether you shall go to the end, whether you will remain passive and remain silent, when the life of my son, who is also your son, is at stake.'[5]

Isaac is saved. A lamb is sacrificed in his place. God re-iterates his Promise. But Abraham is a changed man. He returns alone to his servants. There is the little matter of Hagar and Ishmael.

---

2   Genesis 21:8 – 20

3   Genesis 22:1 – 19

4   Elie Wiesel, *Messengers of God: Biblical Portraits and Legends* (Summit Books, 1976, p. 76)

5   Wiesel, *Messengers of God* (p.91)

There was a test certainly. But what was it about? Did God expect Abraham to argue? To point out that what God demanded he had no right to demand? Was it really about whether Abraham loved God even above the son of the Promise?

Or was something else going on? Did Abraham consider the birth of Ishmael a mistake? Possibly. But God deals in realities, not mistakes. By exiling, and potentially sacrificing both Hagar and Ishmael, Abraham attempted to make two wrongs make a right. What God's direct intervention into Hagar's life revealed to Abraham was that God is not only One, but also a God who saves and frees.

This story is read each Rosh Hashana, Jewish New Year. This festival celebrates the creation of the world, but also marks a day of reckoning. A day each year when God weighs in the scales of his justice the weight of good deeds over bad deeds, and determines what the coming year will bring.

All actions have consequences. Two flowers in a dividing barrier do not themselves bring peace, but they symbolise the necessity of peace and the consequences of our continued disunity as human beings.

The 'shaking reality' of Advent is that it too is a time of reckoning; of letting God weigh in the scales of justice the quality of our relationship to others. A time to remember that, for God, the slave and the child of the slave are as precious as the child of the Promise. Advent is the Christian new year. A time to re-visit how we have followed Jesus in praying for and loving enemies, and making peace.

A Prayer

Ishmael, my brother
How long shall we fight each other?

My brother from times bygone,
My brother - Hagar's son,
My brother, the wandering one.

One angel was sent to us both
One angel watched over our growth -
There in the wilderness, death threatening through thirst,
I a sacrifice on the altar, Sarah's first.

Ishmael my brother, hear my plea
It was the angel that tied thee to me...
Time is running, put hatred to sleep
Shoulder to shoulder, let's water our sheep.

Forms of Prayer for Jewish Worship Vol III,
Prayers for High Holydays

The First Wednesday
God's friend

What is a friend? Elie Wiesel, a survivor of the Holocaust in Europe, says that 'a friend is the person who first makes you aware of your own solitude and his, and helps you escape it so that you, in turn, may help him. It is thanks to him that you can fall silent without shame, and unburden yourself without loss of face.'[1]

Abraham was 'God's friend'. Through good times and bad, each was able to escape their solitude and help the other. God's friendship with Abraham was the key to Abraham's salvation. God knew of Abraham's inconsistencies and contradictions, and sought to help him face and overcome them.

God discerned a man of courage, a survivor. Someone who, despite his moral lapses, fought for a just and united world, and the building of a faithful community. By his willingness to make a path across borders and boundaries, Abraham became the emissary of a new order. With his kinsman Lot, Abraham settled for a while near the cities of Sodom and Gomorrah. These were notorious for their immorality, sexual violence, oppression, and financial corruption.

Despite this, Abraham sought to build within them the foundations of a just society, what came to be called a 'synagogue'. This was not only a place of worship, but a community dedicated to the pursuit of God's justice through the practice of hospitality,

---

1   Noted from Elie Wiesel, *The Gates of the Forest.*

and seeking the welfare of citizens. His efforts appeared to have had little effect.

During one of their conversations, God reveals to Abraham that the cities are to be destroyed.[2] Abraham is outraged. 'Will you really wipe out the good with the bad?' he questions God. Without waiting for an answer he continues, 'Far be it from you to do such a thing to slay the righteous with the wicked … Shall not the Judge of all the Earth do what is just?'

Abraham knew the danger of all-out destruction. He wanted to save both the righteous, and God, from being shamed. He offered his 'friend' help by proposing a bargain. What if 'fifty righteous in the city' can be found, will God save them? God agreed. What about ten - the minimum number for creating a synagogue, the basis of a just society? Again God agreed. Ten were not found. It would take Jesus centuries later to form a righteous community, 'where two or three are gathered together …'.[3]

Despite not finding ten righteous, Abraham knew that strict justice, applied without compassion and mercy, could only end with the destruction of human society. Evil exists in the world, as the story of Sodom and Gomorrah illustrates. Whether the twin cities were destroyed by an 'act of God', or as a consequence of their own sinfulness is not important. The real question that their destruction poses is: how does God face and combat evil?

In James Moll's documentary film *Last Days* the story is told of two girls, Alice and Edith. One night in the barracks of the concentration camp in which they were confined they were whispering about how they used to celebrate *Shabbat* at home. The *kapos* went back and forth, beating anyone who whispered

---

2   Genesis 18:6–19:29

3   Matthew 18:20

during the night. Edith said, 'Why don't we pray? Why don't we pretend we are at home and setting the table? We could do this every Friday night and murmur the Sabbath prayer.'

One Friday morning, standing by the latrine, Edith said, 'It is almost *Shabbat.*' Alice replied, 'Why don't we celebrate inside the latrine? They won't hear us there and we can sing.' The SS never came to the latrine because it was so horrible, she said later. From then on, the girls and other children celebrated Sabbath every week in the latrine at Auschwitz. [4] 'It gave us some kind of normalcy in hell,' said Edith.

This moving story holds a profound truth, that the way we face suffering, even holocaust, determines how we find meaning. These two young women found a way to transform suffering and apparent meaninglessness into prayer, love and song. Despite everything, they resisted evil by transforming it into 'friendship with God'. The deeper meaning of the stories of Abraham, Alice and Edith is that in the 'shaking reality' of Advent those who have friendship with God can learn and know that it is possible to suffer and despair an entire lifetime, and still not give up the hope that one day salvation will come.

Prayer

May the light of God guide us
beyond the limits of our vision.
May the grace of God sustain us,
beyond the limits of our strength.
And may the love of God inspire us
to live abundantly and without limitation.

Anonymous

---

4   This story is adapted from a review in the *Guardian* (22 May 1999).

The First Thursday
Little brothers and sisters

Two Irish *Garda* stood warily by their police car. Pat and I were crossing into what was for them 'No man's land'. We were in Dublin, visiting a small public housing flat in a block scheduled for demolition. The population was being moved out to make space for a luxury development. It was not long before we were accosted by a wary gang of boys demanding to know our business. 'We're going to see the Sisters,' said Pat. Smiles crossed previously uneasy faces and we were accompanied like royalty to the humble dwelling of three 'Little Sisters of Jesus'.

The flat was tiny. The door open. Here was a place of refuge, a safe house where displaced tenants who were yet to be re-housed could meet. Around the kitchen table sat two women in their seventies, a man of indeterminate age who 'needed' community, and a couple of the Sisters. We were a motley crew, with others joining us as the evening went on. All spoke of their anxieties at the break up of their neighbourhood.

Pat, a Roman Catholic priest on furlough from Brazil, visited regularly. As often as not he conducted a simple Eucharist around the communal table. On one occasion a young lad wandered in. Evidently uneasy, he made half-hearted attempts to leave, but never quite made it to the door.

As bread and wine were placed on the table, the boy's language expressed his inner dis-ease: 'What the f… am I doing here?' he said almost to himself. 'Jesus ... I don't even know how to pray.' As the words of the gospel unfolded – 'On the night he was betrayed, Jesus took bread.[1] Pat stopped. Looking around the group he asked, 'Who here has been betrayed?' There was a brief silence. Then for several minutes, stories of betrayal, by partners, friends, the authorities and even the church, poured from the group.

When all who wanted to had spoken, Pat reflected: 'Now you know how it was for Jesus, and Jesus knows how it is for you.' He then invited people to place on the table some token that symbolised or expressed their present situation. One placed a hanky, a symbol of the sense of loss; another a debt notice, still others gestures of their fears and hopes. 'I can't f...ing put anything on. I don't know how to f...ing pray', exclaimed the boy again. 'Then put that on', suggested Pat, 'and whatever else.' The boy appeared to relax a little. When the Eucharist ended he asked, 'Was that f...ing religion?' 'What do you think?' Pat queried. 'If it was,' replied the boy, 'I'm coming back for more.'

The inspiration for this community of misfits came from another misfit, Charles de Foucauld. A man of weak character, he abandoned the woman he had lived with, and sought adventure. In the early days of the twentieth century he joined an expedition to Morocco. One of its aims was to find ways of controlling the region's Muslims, and if necessary killing them.

The expedition experienced many privations, but increasingly de Foucauld grew in his respect and admiration for the piety of Muslims. As he witnessed their prayers, communal life and humanity, he wrote: 'As soon as I discovered there was a God, I understood that I could not do anything other than live for him.'

---

1   Luke 22:14–23

After a profound conversion, like the Christ he came to serve, he ceased to regard Muslims as 'enemies'. He had come to love them.

After a journey through the Holy Land, he returned to the desert. Here he led a contemplative life, living among the poor and campaigning for an end to human trafficking. He sought to set up a community, 'The Little Brothers of Jesus'. Whilst many admired him, no one joined him. On 1 December 1916, amongst a people who had bought him back to faith, he was killed by insurgents.

It was not until 1933 that Charles de Foucauld's vision was to find fulfilment through René Voillaume. All over the world today there are communities of 'Little Brothers' and 'Little Sisters of Jesus', like those I encountered in Dublin. By placing themselves amongst the neglected and discarded of our world, they are sharing - in de Foucauld's words - 'the house of the poor workman who is not sure if tomorrow he will find work and bread, but with all his being shares the suffering of the world'.

The 'shaking reality of Advent' frees us to accept our inconsistencies and let God use us. It is about going where others don't go, and seeing how to do good there. And who knows what we may find? Maybe a lonely boy who doesn't 'know how to f…ing pray', or an activist who 'needs' community, a person of another faith who opens our eyes more clearly, or a couple of courageous elderly women who have seen it all and yet still want to break bread and give thanks to God.

Prayer

Father, I abandon myself into your hands;
do with me what you will.
Whatever you may do, I thank you:
I am ready for all; I accept all.

Let only your will be done in me and all your creatures.
I wish no more than this, O Lord.
Into your hands I commend my soul:
I offer it to you with all the love of my heart.
For I love you, Lord, and so need to give myself,
To surrender myself into your hands,
Without reserve, and with boundless confidence,
For you are my Father.

Charles de Foucauld

The First Friday
'I shall try to help you, God'

Sometimes the most significant encounters in our lives come quite serendipitously. I was introduced to the story of a young Dutch Jewish woman, Etty Hillesum, one spring day in Washington D.C., through a casual encounter with the writer Elisabeth O'Connor. She told me something of Etty's story, of how she died in Auschwitz at the age of twenty-seven. Etty left behind the most extraordinary series of diary writings and notes, revealing a woman of the most intense and rich faith.

It was a cold foggy April day in 2016 when, in the gloom of the Jewish Museum in Amsterdam, I was to catch sight of a small pile of spiral bound notebooks. These were Etty's diaries. One lay open to reveal Etty's distinctive spidery writing. An inner silence descended. I was in the presence of something profoundly sacred. I felt like a pilgrim of old, having arrived at the shrine of some saint or martyr. Inwardly, I knelt in obeisance and gratitude.

During the Nazi occupation of Holland, Etty worked as a clerk with the Jewish Council in Amsterdam. This was an unenviable role because of the deportation of Jews to death camps across Europe.

She knew the destination of the transports from the nearby Westerbork transit camp. Further, she knew that one day she too would be transported.

Etty's family struggled with varying degrees of nervous disability. She too experienced depression, mood swings and physical fatigue. One day, she was introduced to a psychoanalyst, Julius Spier. He provided Etty with strategies for addressing her condition. They became close friends and Etty fell in love with him. Though there are hints that at times the relationship was abusive, Spier introduced her to mysticism and religious experience. He encouraged her to write a record of 'listening to her soul'. What emerged was a remarkable series of diaries.[1]

No reader of Etty comes away unaffected. 'Listening to her soul' we hear the voice of a young woman full of the joys of life, as well as the ambiguities, doubts and questionings that are an integral part of coming to maturity. It is a voice heard against the backdrop of the imminence of deportation, and the near certainty of extermination.

Etty's writings are a dialogue with God. They reveal an intimacy and depth of faith that is both humbling and thought provoking. When her own deportation became inevitable, she offered the following prayer:

> 'I shall promise You one thing, God, one very small thing: I shall never burden my today with cares about my tomorrow, although that takes some practice. Each day is sufficient unto itself. I shall try to help You, God, to stop my strength ebbing away, though I cannot vouch for it in advance. But one thing is becoming increasingly clear to me: that You cannot help us, and that we must help You to help ourselves.

---

1   Ten notebooks of Etty's have survived. Chronologically, the first and seventh are missing. It is widely thought that she took the first book to Auschwitz. Her diaries published as *An Interrupted Life* and *Letters from Westerbork*, have been published in various forms. The most comprehensive is: *Etty - The Letters and Diaries of Etty Hillesum 1941-1943 Complete and Unabridged* (Eerdmans, 2002).

And that is all we can manage these days, and also all that really matters: that we safeguard that little piece of You, God, in ourselves. And perhaps in others as well. Alas, there doesn't seem to be much that You Yourself can do about our circumstances about our lives. Neither do I hold you responsible. You cannot help us, but we must help You and defend Your dwelling place in us to the last.'[2]

Of all the spiritual writing I have read, Etty's has been amongst the most penetrating and influential. The refusal to '*burden my today with cares about tomorrow*' is not simply a notional response to Jesus' exhortation, 'Therefore I tell you, do not worry about your life …'.[3] It is a courageous act, lived against the most extreme of circumstances. Etty's acknowledgement that it '*takes some practice*' is both profoundly realistic, and an antidote to fatalism, despair and hopelessness.

To admit with such candour, '*You, God … cannot help us, but we must help You to help us and defend Your dwelling place in us to the last*', runs counter to today's 'fix everything, God'. With stark realism, Etty points us to the true nature and responsibility of faith. Those of us who claim to experience God are likewise to seek to safeguard '*that little piece of You, God, in ourselves*'. That is what, in Etty's words, '*takes some practice*'.

Etty experienced deep intimacy with God. She believed that '*a kinder day*' would come, though she would not live to see it. Elisabeth O'Connor, who introduced me to Etty, remarked that she comes closest to Jesus in her willingness to put herself in the heart of darkness, all too aware of the consequences. 'Etty's life was not taken from her. She laid it down of her own free accord.

---

2   Etty Hillesum, *An Interrupted Life* (Washington Square Press, 1985)

3   Matthew 6:25

More than anything else, hers is a story of a journey into freedom.'[4] The times in which we live are dark too, and evidence of *a kinder day* coming is in short supply. Advent's 'shaking reality' bids us into a deeper intimacy with God and, like Etty, to seek to *help You* (God) *and defend Your dwelling place in us to the last.*

Prayer

Surrender yourself in all simplicity
the little faith you have is enough.

Brother Roger Schütz of Taizé

---

4   Elisabeth O'Connor, *Cry Pain, Cry Hope* (Word, 1987, p.164)

The First Saturday
Time to wake out of sleep

From the restrictions of his prison cell, and facing certain execution, Alfred Delp reflected: 'There is nothing we modern people need more than to be genuinely shaken up.'[1] Given such circumstances, most of us would consider that our lives had been sufficiently shaken up by being in prison, let alone being condemned to death. Yet Delp showed no sign of self-pity, nor any doubt in God. Neither did he judge others.

What he did was to face a question: 'We may ask God why he has sent us into this time, why he has sent this whirlwind over the earth, why he keeps us in this chaos where all appears hopeless and dark, and why there seems to be no end to this in sight?' It is a question for all of us in Advent.

We are living in times when the very foundations of our society are being shaken. There are wars, and rumours of wars. To use the imagery of the gospels, 'stars are tumbling out of the heavens' and 'constellations' of would-be messiahs offer salvations that can never be realised. Everything that once appeared certain seems to be up in the air, thrown about by diabolical powers that can no longer be controlled.

---

1   All quotations for this chapter from Alfred Delp come from his meditation 'The Shaking Reality of Advent' recorded in *Watch for the Light - Readings for Advent and Christmas* (Orbis, 1981, pp. 82 – 95)

Today political leaders of every hue make promises to 'save' that they cannot keep. The rise of nationalism, the fear of people who are different from us, has led to the lives of minorities across the world being placed under constant threat. Populism has led to the cry that if we keep to our own kind, 'build walls' against the stranger and refugee, tighten legislation, suppress opposition, enhance security forces, then we could be safe.

Such an approach was something that Delp understood: 'We believed that with our own forces we could avert the dangers and banish the night, switch off and halt the internal quaking of the universe. We believed we could harness everything and fit it into a final order that would stand.' These are false securities. The response to such, says Delp, is that 'only when we do not cling to false securities will our eyes be able to see this Last One[2] and get to the bottom of things.'

The 'shaking reality' of Advent for us is that there is no security to be found, save in the Lord who *has, is* and *will* come. It is a time to 'turn away' from false securities of worldly messiahs, in whatever political form they come with their promises to save. Capitalism, nationalism, communism, fascism, populism and all other 'isms' that have promised to 'harness everything and fit it into a final order that will stand,' have been found wanting.

Advent reminds us, in the story of the One who *has, is* and *will* come, that this world is not ours, we occupy it for a brief nanosecond of its life. During this season we can reflect on the transitory nature of our earthly sojourn. The geologist and naturalist Robert Macfarlane bids us contemplate rocks. He says that they provide a 'geological perspective of a past and future that can make human presence, all our loves and nightmares, seem

---

2   Delp means the Coming Christ

irrelevant.'³ The purpose of such reflection, however, is not to avoid engagement with the world and its troubles but, like Delp and others, to find the courage to risk all for the well-being of God's creatures and creation.

'The earth is the Lord's and the fullness thereof' declares the psalmist, and it is an eternal truth. Advent questions all humanity's attempts to appropriate God's gift as its possession. Rather, Advent reminds us that the Lord *has, is* and *will* come to set life in God's order.

Advent forces us to clear from our heads any notion that we are simply in the waiting-room of the final event in the Divine plan. 'We may ask,' as Delp did, 'why God has brought us into this time....' Part of the answer is that we who claim to believe in and follow Christ are to 'arise and wake out of sleep'. Such an awakening means acknowledging how we have been beguiled into trusting 'false' messiahs, clinging to false securities, and believing 'things can only get better'.

Advent reminds us, says Delp, that the 'world today needs people who have been shaken by ultimate calamities and emerged from them with the knowledge and awareness that those who look to the Lord will still be preserved by Him, even if they are hounded from the earth.' We have witnessed such this week in the lives of those we have reflected upon: Hagar, Alice, Edith, Etty, Charles, and Abraham, along with the visionaries striving to build the 'Abraham Path' through divided territories and peoples.

On the eve of the Second Week in Advent, Delp points us towards those whom we traditionally look to in this time: the Prophets. They are the folk who read the signs of the times, and

---

3   I noted this remark of Robert Macfarlane from one of his many books in my Common Place Book - I trust he will forgive me for not remembering which one!

seek to address them, offering both judgment and hope. 'The fact that the Son of man shall come is more than a historic prophecy; it is also a decree that God's coming and the shaking up of humanity are somehow connected.' The challenge for us, as we enter the new week, is to make the connections.

Prayer

Lord, to laugh in the midst of trial
and rejoice in the darkest valley,
is another way of saying: 'Our hope is in You'
Fill us with laughter and joy
whilst we work for peace and strive for justice.

Book of Common Prayer
for Ordinary Radicals

The Second Sunday
The One of peace

Long before dawn we joined the queue at the checkpoint leading from Palestinian Bethlehem into 'no man's land', dividing the City of David from the State of Israel. It was a small act of solidarity. For a few brief minutes we accompanied workers who daily endured the humiliation of being searched and producing passes, prior to crossing to their places of work.

On this Second Sunday in Advent we recall the prophets who foretold the birth of Jesus. Today we light the 'Bethlehem' or 'Candle of peace'. The prophet Micah[1] foretold of the Messiah's birth in Bethlehem, meaning 'house of bread'. From Bethlehem would come the One who would describe himself as 'living bread'. Such moments as we experienced that early morning were an all too salutary reminder of the world's lack of peace, as well as of our incapacity to sit down and break bread together.

The prophets who anticipated God's Messiah were courageous men and women who 'spoke truth to power'. Often at great personal cost they called leaders, peoples and nations to 'seek the things that make for peace'. I was reminded of words from the prophet Isaiah when a few days later I walked through the narrow, bustling market streets of Nazareth. Here, where Jesus grew up, I found myself outside a small church, formerly a synagogue.

1   Micah 5:2

43

Entering the building, widely believed to be some two thousand years old, I wondered if this could really be the place where one Sabbath Jesus took the scroll and began to read from the prophet Isaiah:

> *The Spirit of the Lord God is upon me,*
> *because he has anointed me;*
> *to bring good news to the poor,*
> *He has sent me to proclaim release to the captives*
> *and recovery of sight to the blind,*
> *to let the oppressed go free,*
> *to proclaim the year of the Lord's favour.*[2]

I tend to be sceptical about the authenticity of alleged holy sites. Yet that day I felt that Jesus could have uttered those words in that very place. My spine tingled. Jesus adopted Isaiah's vision for his manifesto, thereby committing himself to fulfilling the promise of the prophets.

As Jesus read Isaiah's words, St Luke records of his hearers that *'all their eyes were fixed upon him'. 'Then',* Luke continued, *'He began to say to them, "Today this scripture has been fulfilled in your hearing". All spoke well of him and were amazed at the gracious words that came from his mouth.'*

In the midst of an anonymous Nazareth congregation on an ordinary Sabbath day stood the One of whom the prophet Micah spoke saying:

> *He shall stand and feed his flock in the strength of the Lord, in the majesty of the name of the Lord his God.*

---

2   Luke 4:18-19 (The longer passage is Luke 4:16-30 - and the Isaiah passage is Isaiah 61:1-9)

And they shall live secure, for now he shall be great to the ends of the earth; and he shall be the one of peace.[3]

For a brief cosmic moment all the things that make for peace came together: *'the One of peace'*: divinely 'anointed', standing and feeding his flock; *the vision of peace*: 'good news to the poor', 'release to the captives', 'sight to the blind', freedom for the 'oppressed'; and the coming of 'jubilee' - 'the year of the Lord's favour'. *The making of peace*: in the manifesto of Jesus, Jubilee, which was traditionally observed every fiftieth year, was now to be lived and worked out daily. The new order would be marked by cancellation of debts, freeing of prisoners, slaves and bonded labourers, the restoration of land to its rightful owners or their successors. Land was to be husbanded to ensure the continuation of fruitful harvests.

In Nazareth, whose name means 'watch tower' or 'new shoot', Jesus was revealed as 'the One of peace'. Jesus as the prophet from the 'house of bread' would be the 'living bread' who would 'feed his flock' with 'new shoots' of peace. Such peace would be evidenced by day-by-day practice of the principles of jubilee. No wonder 'all spoke well of him and were amazed at the gracious words that came from his mouth.'

In the darkness before the dawn, at checkpoints in Bethlehem and across countless borders across the world, it is hard to distinguish between friend and foe. All that can be seen is a common likeness, a shared humanity, yet to be discerned in the light of day. It is something still to be realised. The babe and prophet of Bethlehem still waits to be recognised as the One who offers the only true security and path to peace.

---

3   Micah 5:4–5

All of us long for peace. Jesus understood that peace is something to be learnt and made. We are to be peace *makers*, not simply peace lovers. Advent's 'shaking reality' calls for us to feed from the 'true and living Bread'; set up a 'watch tower' and seek in our own lives 'shoots' of the things that make for peace.

Prayer

Make me a channel of your peace.
Where there is hatred let me bring your love,
where there is injury your pardon, Lord,
where there is doubt, true faith in you.

From a Prayer of St Francis of Assisi

The Second Monday
Left unsaid

Most of us have experienced times when we recognise that it is better to leave something unsaid. Sometimes it is a 'bite one's tongue' moment - one of those times when words said in anger, self-justification or defence could have caused an outcome and division that simply was not worth it.

Yet there are times when leaving things unsaid can be provocative. It was not so much what Jesus said in the Nazareth synagogue as he laid out his vision of *shalom* - peace with justice - but what he left unsaid. Initially his hearers received what he said as 'gracious words' - a kind of cosmic moment of opportunity for peace. But suddenly things turned nasty. The congregation quickly became a mob. Bundling Jesus out of the synagogue, they swept him through the town and threatened to throw him over a cliff.

How do we account for such a mood change? Was it because Jesus spoke of good news to the poor, release to captives, sight to the blind, freedom for the oppressed, or the inauguration of perpetual jubilee? Would not such blessings be welcomed by a people whose history was littered with the realities of poverty, oppression, captivity and debt?

The devout, albeit volatile synagogue community often heard those words from Isaiah. They knew them well. Like many of us in church, words so easily go over our heads, and too late we realise something important has happened. So it was for the Nazareth

47

congregation. It took a moment to realise: something had been left unsaid. In yesterday's reflection we read words from St Luke's gospel. These were the words Jesus used. But he read them from the text of Isaiah[1] and they say something *slightly* different:

The Spirit of the Lord is upon me, because he has anointed me; he has sent me to bring good news to the oppressed, to bind up the broken hearted,
To proclaim liberty to captives, and release to the prisoners, to proclaim a year of the LORD's favour, and the day of vengeance of our God.

Did you spot the missing key words? Jesus had left out the phrase '*and the day of vengeance of our God*'. Was it an oversight? Did he lose concentration? Or was it deliberate? As they woke up to what Jesus had not said, they concluded his omission was no accident.

In the popular mind Isaiah's words were exclusively for God's chosen people. The promise of a Deliverer - a *Messiah* - was deep in the national psyche. The Coming One would bring God's payback time. God would exact retribution for all the injustices, persecution, oppression and other calumnies committed against the Chosen Ones through the ages.

Yet by leaving out the phrase *the day of vengeance*, it seemed that Jesus was raising a question mark over the promises of payback and retribution for all the wrongs that the Chosen people had suffered. What's more, Jesus gave God's imprimatur to what had been read by adding the claim: '*Today this scripture has been fulfilled in your hearing.*'

Through an apparently innocuous amending of the text, Jesus revealed the true nature of God's purpose in becoming human. There are to be no more elites, no more 'chosen ones', no more

---

1   Isaiah 61:1–3

outsiders, no more enemies. There is to be no more vengeance, no more 'getting our own back'. And to give additional emphasis to his message, he reminded his hearers of the stories of two acts of mercy offered by the prophets Elijah and Elisha towards Gentile outsiders.[2]

The core of Jesus' new order is healing, forgiveness and the making of peace with justice. His words previously perceived as *gracious* are now received as threatening. Jesus reveals that the Messiah is not come for an exclusive 'chosen' people. The Messiah comes too for the immoral, the violent, the oppressors of God's 'chosen ones'. As the truth dawned on the Nazareth community, it was simply too much to take.

Anger is often described as a 'secondary emotion', because it is nearly always an expression of something deeper. Fear, hurt, anxiety, threat and loss are often the primary causes. What made the Nazareth congregation angry was their fear at losing their unique status. If Jesus interpreted God right, then no longer would they have exclusive access to God's love, mercy and justice. Now they would be just like 'them others'. St James was to write later: 'God's saving justice is never served by human anger.'[3] Perhaps we should not be surprised at their anger.

Accompanying workers through the checkpoint in Bethlehem exposed the division between Palestinians and Israelis. Yet somehow it was symptomatic of all our divisions. What the rejection of Jesus in Nazareth reveals is our ongoing refusal to see all humanity as God's children. The 'shaking reality' of Advent is that the salvation Jesus brings is the restoration of the fullness of our humanity physically, socially, spiritually. Receiving such

2   1 Kings 17:1–24 ; 2 Kings 5

3   James 1:20 New Jerusalem Bible.

salvation, and following Jesus, offers the possibility for creating a society in which justice, mercy and peace are experienced by all.

Prayer

In your mercy and compassion
walk with us as we continue our journey of healing
to create a future that is just and equitable.
Lord you are our hope.

National Aboriginal and Torres Strait Islanders
Ecumenical Commission, 2003 Prayer

The Second Tuesday
I am about to take my life into my hands

The story of Esther is one of the lesser-known biblical tales. It tells of a Jewish woman exiled with her people in Babylon. Captive and humiliated, their very identity and existence threatened, Esther nevertheless comes to be respected by her captors. Her rise to influence is as a consequence of an unseemly, and by today's standards sexist, beauty competition.

The King of Persia was seeking the most beautiful woman in the land to be his consort. His courtiers scoured the land for suitable candidates, preparing them for their eventual assessment by the king. On seeing Esther, it is reported that 'the king loved Esther more than all the other women ... She won his favour and devotion'.[1]

The Book of Esther is unusual in that it tells us nothing about Jewish rituals or structures. The assimilation of the exiles seems complete. No one speaks of the Promised Land, nor of any hope of return. Prophets, priests and kings - apart from the Persian king - are not mentioned. Yet Esther and her companions have a profound sense of the presence and power of God. The author

---

1   Esther 2:17.The story of Esther is recounted in the Bible in two sections. The first is in a short version in the Old Testament. The second in an extended form is to be found in the Inter-Testamental books known as the Apocrypha. The whole story is worth reading. It reads like a good novel.

seems to point us to the wider truth that Israel's God is not bound by tribe or territory.

Despite their captivity, the Jews seemed to enjoy the respect of the gentile community. In exile they lived quietly and unobtrusively. It was not to remain so. Dark clouds were on the horizon, and their silence would not protect them. Rivalries and power struggles in the king's court would threaten not only the lives of Esther and the assimilated Jews, but eventually the king himself.

Mordechai was among a small coterie of Jews in the king's court. Esther trusted him as both a confidante and adviser. However, Mordechai had a rival at court. His name was Haman, a man described as having 'precedence over all the king's Friends. So all at court used to do obeisance to Haman, for so the king had commanded to be done.'[2] Jewish religion forbade obeisance to anyone but God. Knowing this, Haman inveigled the king to sign an act of genocide into law, allowing the execution of any who refused to offer obeisance.

Despite being the king's 'Friend', Haman was secretly plotting his assassination. Between them, Esther and Mordechai discovered the plot, though initially they did not associate it with Haman. The king was warned by Haman of the threat, but ascribed it to the Jews, and Mordechai in particular. At Haman's request, the king issued an injunction for Mordechai to be hanged.

Mordechai was doomed unless Esther could help. Until that moment, Esther had kept her Jewish identity hidden from the king. Mordechai warned her that her silence would not spare her. Despite her status and intimacy with the king, entering his presence was akin to having access to a god. Only the 'king's Friends' and a few favoured courtiers could assume such a privilege. Whilst

---

2   Esther 3:1–3.

Esther's status and the king's love for her placed her in such company, the king was notoriously fickle, given to paranoia and despotic acts. Even for Esther the risk of intercession was great, not least because of the king's injunction against the Jews.

Recalling the tradition of her forebears in times of crisis, Esther began a period of fasting and prayer. Removing her royal apparel, make-up and perfumes, she covered her head with ashes and dung. Praying to the Lord God of Israel, she said: '*O my Lord, you only are our king; help me, who am alone and have no helper but you, and am about to take my life into my hands.*'[3]

Esther's prayer was urgent and full of faith. The suffocating atmosphere of the court, and the circumstances faced by Mordechai and other Jews, made her prayer a profound act of defiance. Refusing to give in to despair, she bravely faced reality: 'I am alone and have no helper but God.' Her decision to act was made in the full knowledge that, in her words, 'I am about to take my life into my hands.'

Esther's act of fasting, praying and humility before God are vital preparation for her encounter with the king, and her intercession for Mordechai's life. 'You only are our king,' she prays. By so doing, she seeks grace to conquer her fears and sense of isolation. What she proposes carries huge risk. Despite the private nature of her prayer, its outcome will take her to the heart of despotic, un-predictable power. She is literally taking her life into her hands in order to save Mordechai.

Few of us face such risk and danger. Yet Advent's 'shaking reality' reminds us that our salvation places upon us a responsibility to be advocates and defenders of those who are in the hands of 'evil doers'. Esther knew that without her intervention, violence

---

3   Esther 14:2–4, New Jerusalem Bible.

would break out and her people would be destroyed. 'All it takes for evil to triumph is for good people to do nothing', is a widely quoted aphorism. But it is true.

Esther was not a prophet, but she had prophetic intent. A prophet is one who reads the signs of the times and seeks to address them through prayer and action. Taking her life into her hands, she worshipped the Lord in the beauty of holiness through her courage and witness. Advent's shaking reality bids us do the same. Esther's intercession paid off. Haman was exposed as duplicitous, and was hanged on the gallows prepared for Mordechai.

Prayer

O Lord God of Abraham, O God whose might is over all, hear the voice of my despairing and save us from the hands of evil doers. And save me from my fear.

Esther

The Second Wednesday
And save me from my fear

A late evening phone call interrupted me while I was writing an early draft of this reflection. A friend of mine who has been committed to building peace in Northern Ireland following the Good Friday Agreement is afraid for her life. She has spent many years, along with other groups and individuals, seeking to create frameworks for mediation and peace-building amongst former enemies and rivals.

Such engagement has not been easy. Mutual suspicion, latent hatreds, and desire for revenge, have bedeviled the work of reconciliation. Those engaged in mediation have frequently found themselves threatened, or caught up in events and circumstances beyond their control. Truth-telling and trust have often been overwhelmed by lies and deceit. My friend's fear had been caused through the discovery of a link between a suspected assassination attempt and a community organisation of which she was a trustee.

Her concern was not about what she should do; that much was clear. What exercised her, as it would any of us, was that she was afraid of what could happen to her if she did what she knew she should do. Her fear was well grounded. Prior to the peace agreement, attacks had taken place on people who had 'grassed' on perpetrators of wrong-doing.

When Esther prayed, 'help me, who am alone, and have no helper but you, and am about to take my life into my hands', she concluded by saying: 'And save me from my fear'. Few of us escape from a sense of fear when we confront difficult, risky and dangerous decisions. Most of us are spared circumstances as dramatic as those faced by Esther or my friend, but we know the debilitating power of fear. In order to act and do what is right, we too need to be 'saved' from paralysing fear.

As we talked on the phone, I shared the story of Esther. I reflected too on the example of others who had influenced, inspired and encouraged me in times of fear and doubt. One of these was the late Mother Mary Clare. During the Second World War, Mary Clare served as a nurse in Cardiff, South Wales. It was a city that was being heavily bombed by the Nazis. With her fellow citizens she spent many hours in bomb shelters, emerging only when the 'All Clear' siren sounded.

It was a terrifying time. The damage, death and injuries that people faced in the aftermath of the raids were truly horrific. For each person who survived the destruction of other people's lives, the unspoken question arose: Might it be me next time? Mary Clare often found herself praying, 'Lord keep me safe'. One day it dawned on her that such a prayer was both unrealistic and inappropriate. Why should God protect her and not another of his creation, she reasoned. Like Esther facing the reality and risks of her situation, she concluded that whilst she could not pray for safety, she could instead ask God to make her brave.

Mary Clare and Esther refused to escape their responsibility for situations that were frightening and life-threatening. Both faced the truth that God does not save people from realities because they believe and trust in Him. What they demonstrated was that God does change situations through people of faith and courage by strengthening them and removing paralysing fear.

What such people reveal is a willingness to face situations that appear impossible to change, but when viewed with the eye of faith allow God to break in and renew hope. 'Hope is believing in spite of the evidence, and watching the evidence change', observed the public theologian Jim Wallis.

Esther and Mother Mary Clare knew that they were holding in their hands not only their own lives, but the lives of others. Both testified to the truth that, if they lived paralysed by fear, then their actions were more likely to lead to cowardice than bravery. Not for nothing does the Bible re-iterate the phrase 'Fear not' more times than any other single instruction.

Fear un-addressed can make us act counter to our faith in Jesus Christ. It can make us defensive, cause us to act prejudicially towards those whom Christ calls us to love and serve: the poor, the weak, the stranger, the imprisoned and discriminated against. In times of trial and anxiety, fear affects us all. Facing my own fear in situations where courage and faith have been required, I have found resolve and courage from these words in *The Book of Common Prayer* Evening Prayer:

> O God, from whom all holy desires, all good counsels, and all just works do proceed; Give unto thy servants that peace which the world cannot give; that both our hearts may be set to obey thy commandments, and also that by thee we being *defended from the fear of our enemies*[1] may pass our time in rest and quietness; through the merits of Jesus Christ our Saviour.

Before putting down the phone that night, my friend and I talked and together prayed the Evening Collect. When I called her next

---

1   Parentheses mine

day, she had made the words of Esther's prayer, 'save me from my fear' - and the Collect's defended from the fear of our 'enemies', her own. She spoke of how she had been delivered, slept well, and found new resolve, as well as fresh trust in God to see her through whatever might befall her. She had discovered again the 'shaking reality' of the Advent Christ who *has* come, *is* come, and *will come again.*

The Second Thursday
Signs of the prophets

Some years ago I lay in a hospital bed following heart surgery. I had received a letter from my friend Pat who worked in the *favelas* of São Pãolo in Brazil. In his letter he told me he would ask the slum dwellers to pray for my recovery. 'I always tell them,' he said, 'that there is great power in their prayer, because it comes from so much faith.'

Pat recounted a conversation he had had with a woman under a graffiti-ridden subway. She had come in from the countryside to visit her daughter, who had been knocked down and badly injured by a lorry. Her nine-month-old granddaughter had been killed outright. The woman journeyed for thirteen days. She walked, but took lifts when they were offered. She often went hungry, accepting food when it was given. She slept, she said, along the roadside, in hedges, fields, petrol stations and shop doorways.

'How did you go through such hardship?' Pat asked her. Casting her eyes upwards to the underside of the subway, she raised her hands and said: 'Isn't God our Father? And isn't Mary our mother?' 'What can anyone say to that?' wondered Pat. 'I was once again reduced to silence, to a profound reflection on my own ignorance and my own ever so fragile faith. My habit of neatly circumventing the risk of a more authentically committed simplicity.' He concluded, 'Thank God for those apostles, prophets, pilgrims, anonymous angels of hope hidden away under bridges, unknown and rejected by the symbols of progress that roar by them triumphantly, all the day.'

On a subsequent visit to São Pãolo I met with a small group of professional people who had committed themselves to seek the welfare of the poor. Together they sought to live simply, raising consciousness of the plight of those in the slums amongst their well-to-do neighbours.

Over a simple meal, the group shared their vision and story. A Lent course entitled 'God's Preferential Option for the Poor' had caused them to question their comfortable, self-sufficient lives, disconnected from the mass of the urban poor. The course had challenged them to do something about it. They agreed to meet regularly, to read, pray and meditate upon the gospels and the Book of Acts. Together they reflected on what the implications of making 'a preferential option for the poor' might mean for their common future.

After some weeks they concluded that they could share their income, live more simply, and dedicate time to the welfare of others. 'Each of us seeks to live on ten percent of what we earn, and we use the rest to further our work,' one person told me. 'We try to avoid consumerism, new cars, the latest gadgets and clothes. We try not to say "no" to any need presented to us, and be open and available to meet each other's needs.'

This had been no flash in the pan. I met the group in its twentieth year of serving others. Their range of engagement included an education centre for sixty street children. Here food, shelter, a place of protection from sex traffickers and the police, were offered. The police often treated street children, in their words, as 'vermin to be shot'. Even as we spoke that day a report came in of one of the children being the victim of such a shooting.

What affected me most deeply was the clarity of the group's logic. Living simply meant there was not so much to maintain or obtain. Sharing their resources offered hope and new life to others, as well as freedom from anxiety to them as a group. They continued having meetings for prayer, study of Scripture, and sharing common meals. These times of *koinonia* prepared them for the task of lobbying authorities, engagement in legal action, and the ongoing re-shaping of their lives amongst those they were called to serve.

In her wonderful book, *The Zookeeper's Wife*,[1] Diane Ackerman reminds us of the meaning in Hebrew word for prophet - *navi*. This she says combines three processes: *navach* which means 'to cry out' ; *nava* - meaning 'to gush, or flow', and *navuv* - 'to be hollow'. The task of mediation, Ackerman observed, is 'to open the heart, to unclog the channel between the infinite and the mortal'.

Today's prophets are those who 'cry out' from the depths of faith, often in the midst of poverty, like signs on subway walls. From such 'gush' and 'flow' lives together with words of hope. People 'hollowed out' by the realities of life, nevertheless become vessels able to receive the Divine love poured out in the Advent of the One who *has, is* and *will come*. The 'shaking reality' calls us to resistance and to hope in response to Jesus who said: 'Inasmuch as you have acted justly towards the least of these sisters and brothers of mine, you have acted justly towards me.'[2]

Prayer

> Lord, help me to arrange my life
> according to the principle

---

1   Diane Ackerman, *The Zookeepers Wife - A True Story of an Unlikely Heroine* (Headline, 2013). I have slightly adapted her presentation to fit in with the text

2   Matthew 25:45, my paraphrase

which counsels us to hold to the difficult,
because everything alive holds to it;
so then that which now seems most alien
will become what we most trust,
and find most faithful.
For this reason it will not cease to be difficult,
but for this reason it will not cease to grow.

Based on words of Rainer Maria Rilke

The Second Friday
Sanctity and sacramentality of life

Choosing Christmas cards each year presents my wife and me with a challenge: how can we step beyond the apparently predictable and sentimental, as we seek to offer the season's compliments to family, friends and colleagues? Over the years our search has taken us into the company of artists whose work has some something of a 'shaking reality' about it. Among these have been a trinity of artist prophets whose work has distilled profound truths and reminders of what it means to welcome Christ at Christmas.

Fritz Eichenberg, Käthe Kollwitz and Ade Bethune have produced works that speak out of their experience into a world big on despair and short on hope. Eichenberg and Kollwitz were Germans, and Ade Bethune, an American. Eichenberg came from an assimilated Jewish background and escaped the pogroms in Europe to the United States. Käthe Kollwitz was an internationally regarded lithographer and sculptor between the First and Second World Wars. Under the Nazi regime, she was subject to a banning order, and threatened with internment in a concentration camp.

Fritz Eichenberg was an artist who specialised in woodcuts. Once in the United States of America, he became a Quaker. He was strongly influenced by co-founder of the *Catholic Worker* Dorothy Day in New York. He contributed much of his art, chiefly wood engravings, to the movement's weekly paper.

His poignant and powerful images reflected the life of Christ amongst the poor, oppressed and war-torn.

'It is my hope,' wrote Eichenberg. 'that in some small way I have been able to contribute to peace through compassion, and also to the recognition, as George Fox[1] has said ... That there is that of God in everyone, a conception of the sanctity of human life which precludes all war and violence.'

In a leafy suburb of Berlin there is a gallery dedicated to the work of Käthe Kollwitz. Kollwitz lost her son Peter in the First World War, when he was killed in the trenches. His death struck her 'like a thunderbolt', she said. In one lithograph in the museum there is an image of a mother protecting her children entitled *Seed for sowing should not be milled*. It was drawn in 1938 as a warning against Germany's growing militarisation.

In the aftermath of her son's death, Kollwitz sculpted her most famous piece: *Mother with her Dead Son*. By 1939 the Nazis had banned her work. She died a few days prior to the signing of Germany's surrender in 1945. Today in the Neue Wache in Berlin her powerful sculpture 'to victims of war and dictatorship' stands as her memorial. Kollwitz's passion for a just and equal society was coupled with a pacifism that went beyond 'just anti-war'. She passionately believed that 'A new idea will arise and there will be an end to wars.' She acknowledged that it was a conviction that would demand much hard work, but that one day its time would come.

Ade Bethune was a nineteen-year-old art student when she learned of the *Catholic Worker* movement in New York. On spec she sent a picture to Dorothy Day, the movement's founder. It was of an angry innkeeper shaking his fists as he evicts Mary and Joseph from the inn at Bethlehem. Day was to describe Bethune's

---

1   George Fox was one of the founders of the Society of Friends - the 'Quakers'

work as possessing 'a sense of sacramentality of life, the goodness of things'.

Eichenberg's *Christmas 1954* depiction of Mary with her new-born baby lying on a simple bed in the midst of the city could so easily be drawn today. Cattle lean over a makeshift fence; Joseph, lantern in hand, gazes with perplexed wonder, while shepherds stand with hats removed in respectful homage, the whole scene set against a background of tower blocks. Above them, a star, a dove and angels gather, images of hope and peace. Yet beneath the cot in which Mary and her child sleep are gathered leviathans, dragons and pigs. With sleepless eye they wait to devour the exhausted mother and her offspring.

Such images shake a reality into the schmaltz and sentimentality that clog this season of expectation. They dare us to think differently about what it means to embrace and welcome the Coming One as 'Prince of Peace'. Their message, whilst being uncomfortable, as with all prophets, nevertheless offers hope. But it is a hope dependent upon courage and faith that a new future is possible. Eichenberg calls us to embrace the sanctity of life, which precludes all war and violence, because 'there is that of God in everyone'. Kollwitz calls us to resist the prevailing world view and welcome 'a new idea … [that] there will be an end to all wars' into our hearts and lives. Ade Bethune bids us become 'The saints (who) are Christ', knowing that, like Mary and Joseph, we must face the possibility of losing the world's hospitality, whilst not losing sight of the sacramentality of life and goodness of things.

Prayer

May the radical justice of God the Father,
the liberating forgiveness of God the Son,

the revolutionary transforming presence of
God the Holy Spirit, so blow through our lives,
that we follow Christ into this broken world,
bringing saving justice to all.

Attributed to Chris Sugden

'Love, and say it with your life.'

St Augustine

The Second Saturday
Cries in the wilderness

'Woe to an age when the voices of those who cry in the wilderness have fallen silent,' declared Alfred Delp from his prison cell, 'outshouted by the noise of the day, or swallowed up in the intoxication of progress, or growing smothered and fainter for fear and cowardice.' With these words Delp began his reflection on John the Baptist, the one who cries in the wilderness.

Whilst preparing this reflection, I heard the voice of Fergal Keane coming from the television, a BBC Reporter of immense humanity and compassion. Once more he was in a conflict zone, bearing testimony to the risk of famine, of children dying, and a relentless killing machine deployed by the government. This had led to a refusal to allow the passage of humanitarian aid, and the indiscriminate use of weapons whose supply conditions had been callously ignored.

Keane appears as a John the Baptist-like figure. Throughout years of reporting from the world's most troubled places he has been 'a crying voice raising plaint and accusation'. Reporting humanity's inhumanity through the years has taken its personal toll, but with immense courage and insight Keane has returned to the fray, appearing to accept that if to be 'one who cries in the wilderness', is his vocation, then he must remain faithful.

I have never met Fergal Keane, but I have had the privilege of meeting and sharing work with the photographer Don McCullin.[1] For sixty years McCullin has recorded tales of war, starvation, and inhumanity that would crush the spirit. Some years ago we worked together on the installation of a sculpture in the grounds of the Bishop's Palace in Wells. It was of Josefina de Vasconcellos's work, *The Weight of our Sins*, originally designed for UNICEF. The sculpture was of children carrying a cross, burdened down by the weight of humanity's sins against them. All this, and more, McCullin had seen.

Covering the 'Dirty Wars' in Latin America in the 1980s and 1990s, Mev Puleo described her work as letting 'the camera lens [be] the eye of my soul, through which I touch the world, and the world touches me'. I'd heard McCullin express a similar outlook. Puleo questioned whether she dare invade lives, and steal moments from people. Yet all the time she seemed to bear a moral responsibility to share such encounters with the world, to be a voice for them, and expose their humanity in the midst of inhumanity.

For people who have witnessed so much inhumanity, questions about God, the meaning of life, the future of hope inevitably arise. Despite their apparent un-answerability, what arises in such witnesses is a profound and deep compassion. Like John the Baptist, they are a voice in the wilderness, crying.

Delp believed from the heart of darkness that 'not for an hour can life dispense with these John the Baptist characters ... these original individuals, struck by the lightning of mission and vocation ... [whose] heart goes out before them ... their eye is so clear-sighted ... their judgment so incorruptible'. With whatever

---

1   Now Sir Don McCullin, he was knighted in the 2017 New Year Honours List

voice is given to them, 'They cry for blessing and salvation', says Delp. 'They summon us to our last chance, while already they feel the ground quaking and the rafters creaking and see the firmest of mountains tottering inwardly and see the very stars in heaven hanging in peril.' Yet such people carry with them a deep sense of being insignificant - 'the least' amongst humanity. It is as if they have grasped wordlessly a truth that cannot be expressed.

'There is none greater than John the Baptist,' answered Jesus to the question by disciples of the imprisoned John: 'Are you the one who is to come, or are we to wait for another?' Still having access to John's cell, Jesus instructs the disciples to tell him, 'what you have seen and heard; the blind receive their sight, the lame walk, the lepers are cleansed, the deaf hear, the dead are raised, the poor have good news brought to them. And blessed is anyone who takes no offence at me.'[2] Then turning to the crowd, Jesus declared, 'Yet the least in the Kingdom is greater than he is.'[3]

With these surprising words Jesus presented a disturbing truth to those who wanted their religion exclusive, private and shaped by 'do's and don'ts'. Jesus upheld as 'great' in the Kingdom of God those who believe they have no significance, are often unsure about God, yet their very lives epitomise God's saving justice. They are truly great, for they expose injustice and inhumanity and open the door to God's wider purpose of restoring humanity to wholeness.

On the eve of this Third Week of Advent, Delp invites us to reflect on 'Cries in the Wilderness.' Amongst these I see Fergal Keane, Don McCullin and Mev Puleo, who face the 'shaking

---

2   Luke 7:22–23

3   Luke 7:28

reality' because their 'heart has gone out before them', and 'who do not cry for the sake of crying or for the sake of the voice'.

Prayer

O Lord, today we know once more, and in quite practical terms, what it means to clear away the rubble and make paths smooth again.
We will have to know it and do it for years to come.
Let the crying voices ring out, pointing out the wilderness and overcoming the devastation from within.
May the Advent figure of John, the relentless envoy and prophet in
God's name, be no stranger in our wilderness of ruins.
For how shall we hear unless someone cries out
above the tumult of destruction and delusion?

Alfred Delp

The Third Sunday
To guide our feet

Forming a picture of John the Baptist from the various pieces of gospel text is a bit like trying to make a 3D jigsaw puzzle. Each author has their own agenda with regard to John. St Luke fills us in with the substance of the picture, telling us about his parentage, his birth, his hearers and his message. St Matthew focuses too on his hearers and their response to his message. St Mark is quite matter of fact concerning his message and his ritual of baptising. John concentrates on the debate between the religious authorities, on who Jesus is, and what right he has to say what he is saying, and do what he is doing. Where all the writers are agreed is that John is a signpost to 'One who will come'.

John was descended from a priestly family. His father Zechariah was one of a community of priests who ministered in the Temple in Jerusalem. His mother Elizabeth was a cousin of Mary of Nazareth, the woman who was to be the mother of Jesus. Elizabeth in the language of the time was 'barren'. Lack of fertility was rarely ascribed to males.

Selected by drawing lots, Zechariah is in the inner sanctuary of the Temple, offering incense as prayer to the Lord, when he is visited by a messenger from God, Gabriel. Unsurprisingly, Zechariah is 'startled and overcome by fear', as St Luke tells us. 'Do not be afraid,' continues the angel. 'Your prayer has been heard, your wife Elizabeth will bear a son and you will name him

John. His birth will fill you with joy and delight and he will bring gladness to many'.

Without waiting for a response, the angelic messenger proceeds to outline what the now named 'John' will *be* and *do*. In terms of *being*, he will '*be* great in the eyes of the Lord'. He will *be* an ascetic, forswearing wine and strong drink; and he will '*be* filled with the Holy Spirit from his birth'.

What he will *do* is 'bring back many … to the Lord their God'. He will act as a 'fore-runner, possessed by the spirit and power of Elijah', one the folk heroes of the Jewish people. In addition, he will 'reconcile father and child … convert the rebellious to the ways of the righteous' and 'prepare a people that shall be fit for the Lord'.

Zechariah is, in modern parlance, gobsmacked. He does not know whether to believe or not. Struck dumb by the departing angel, Zechariah is told he will not speak until the child has been born. And so it came to pass - Elizabeth conceived, the child is born, all the family and friends 'share delight' in the 'kindness of the Lord'. On the eighth day after his birth, at the ceremony of circumcision, he is to be named 'Zechariah' - after his dad. Still dumb, Zechariah asks for a chalk board and writes 'His name is John' - and his tongue is untied, and he speaks. Uttering a prophecy - he pronounces over the new-born:

> You, my child, will be called the prophet of the Most High …
> leading his people to a knowledge of salvation, through the forgiveness of their sins …
> For in the tender compassion of our God, the dawn from on high shall break upon us, to shine on those who live in darkness, under the shadow of death, and to guide our feet into the way of peace.

Whew! What an introduction. What expectation. What next? Well, surprisingly nothing. Luke after all that build-up simply says: 'As the child grew up he became strong in spirit; he lived out in the desert before he publicly appeared before Israel.' End of. But is it? Are there clues here? Is the writer hinting at a certain rebelliousness with his phrase 'he became strong in spirit'? Given the attitude he was to take to the religious elite, and they to him, was he turning his back on the formality of religion with its regulations, rituals and compromises?

Possibly. Another set of pieces of the jigsaw which hint at such are to be found in the gospel of St John. Seemingly out of nowhere, John appears at a place in the desert which he locates as 'Bethany beyond the Jordan'. For us, such a locality seems inconsequential, but not to John's readers. This is a place that is significant for two reasons. Firstly, it was the legendary site of Elijah's passing on the mantle to his successor, Elisha. Hence John's dress - a coat of camel hair, and his food - locusts and wild honey, are both reminiscent of the ascetic Elijah.

Second, the wilderness was territory outside of the Promised Land, the land of the covenant. In Hebrew the word for wilderness means 'a place of those cut off, or driven out'.[1] Such a location was outside the jurisdiction of the Temple and the religious authorities. It was regarded as uninhabitable and a place of evil spirits. Yet the presence of scribes and Pharisees in such a place indicated the sense of threat to their authority and power felt by them because of John's words and actions.

Whatever contribution to the jigsaw of knowledge about John the evangelists make, their common witness is to John as the forerunner of One who is to come: 'One mightier', say Matthew,

---

1   The word is *midbar*

Mark and Luke, whilst St John uses the imagery 'Lamb of God', reflecting a term in common parlance for a conquering hero. Jesus will situate his mission among the 'cut off' and the 'driven out'. He will, like John, make his mark beyond the boundaries of religious jurisdiction that confines and compromises. From the wilderness he will bring a justice that comes to life, where feet can be guided 'into the way of peace', and people become 'fit for the Lord'.

The 'shaking reality' of Advent calls us to move away from the barren-ness and infertility of despair. To breathe again the air where God can be freed to bring new life, reconciliation, health and peace. Like John, our characters are complex and multi-faceted. Like Zechariah, we too can be unbelieving, and were an angel of God to appear before us with promises we too would be struck dumb. Advent provides us with our own mini desert, where we can stand outside all the tradition, expectation and consumerism - and allow God's conquering hero to appear before us, to inspire, nurture and comfort us. So today we light the pink candle - known as the *Gaudete* - or 'joy' candle. We do so in hope, like Elizabeth, Mary and yes, even Zechariah.

Prayer

Lord, you called your servant John the Baptist
to prepare the way for the Christ to come,
and to guide your people in the way of peace.
So today, you call us to prepare for Christ's coming,
and to be instruments of your peace.
Grant us wisdom and courage to heed your call,
and to follow you.

The Third Monday
Repent ... the kingdom is near

Just as it is beginning to look a lot like Christmas, the Advent liturgy confronts us with John the Baptist. It would be safe to say that he is not your average fun guy. For a start he seems to prefer his own company, and even that in remote places. Dressed in camel's skin, and with a diet of locusts and wild honey, he would be rare company at the Christmas party with turkey and all the trimmings.

John's language is terse, cryptic, and distinctly judgmental. Yet, despite his disturbing image and uncomfortable message, he draws the crowds. Love him or hate him, adherents and enemies leave the security of the cities and towns for the aridity of the desert, to listen to him. In time his cousin Jesus will offer him the ultimate accolade: 'There is none greater than John the Baptist.'

Given all this, perhaps there is a reason for turning aside from the carols and mince pies to reflect on why such an individual invades our space today. To understand both John and Jesus requires us to know something of the times in which they lived. Their homeland was an occupied territory governed by the Romans. The Romans ruled through locally appointed kings, known as 'tetrarchs',[1] all of whom belonged to a single extended family - the 'Herods'.

---

[1] 'Tetrarch' means a 'quarter'. The Herods ruled small jurisdictions within Palestine.

The Herodian dynasty ruled in conjunction with the religious elite, who maintained the Temple and synagogue systems. Together they headed up a kind of theocracy.[2] The emperor of Rome was regarded as a god. Such a concept was deeply alien and offensive to Judaism. However, in return for the delivery of *Pax Romana* within Palestine, the Romans were prepared to allow Temple and synagogue worship, together with the administration of religious and civil laws. The interpretation and application of 'God's law' lay with the priests.

The influential and wealthy comprised some five per cent of the population. The majority of the rest can be described with the generic term 'poor'. The gospel writers each focus on a dimension of poverty. St Mark uses a term that can be translated, 'disenfranchised masses'. St Luke speaks of the 'little ones' - the despised, women, children - who have been called 'those who cringe'. St Matthew focuses on the economically needy. St John's agenda is on those who are disempowered through lack of education and influence.

The relationship between rulers and ruled was fragile. Rome feared rebellion, and there had been many local uprisings that had been put down with ruthless efficiency. Every such act risked the 'arrangement' between the Judean rulers and the Empire. So the rulers, both civil and spiritual, kept a tight grip on the ninety-five per cent of the population who were their subjects. As so often, what kept a fractious elite together was their common fear of the mass of the people.

Into the maelstrom of dis-ease and oppressive power came John the Baptist. For centuries the prophetic voice had been silent.

---

2   Theocracy is a form of government in which a deity is the source from which all authority derives

The last voice heard was that of Malachi - the 'messenger' - with a promise from God: 'Lo, I will send you the prophet Elijah before the great and terrible day of the Lord comes.'[3] Though there has been much debate over the identity of Elijah, most agree that John the Baptist fulfils the criteria, even if it can be subsequently applied to others.

John is to 'Prepare the way of the Lord'. He is the 'voice of one crying in the wilderness'[4] - both literally and metaphorically -'making a straight highway' for God's anointed to arrive. From his eyrie in the desert John gathers people at the banks of the Jordan river. His message is simple, stark, clear cut: 'Repent, for the kingdom of heaven has come near.'[5] Those who receive it, John baptises.

The majority who come to the Jordan are the disenfranchised and powerless. But John's message and his impact worry the authorities, and representatives of the religious elite who view it all with increasing anxiety. To these Pharisees and Sadducees John speaks in particularly scathing language: 'You brood of vipers! Who warned you of the wrath to come?'

John critiques their religious heritage, and by implication their 'arrangement' with the pagan power and the Herodian dynasty. Dramatically he warns that 'the axe is laid to the root of the trees …' The time of 'de-cision' - cutting away - has come. For the religious elite the 'cut' will be deep. Can they say 'no' to empire, to privilege and power? Can they line up with the 'confused majority', the 'not needed', the 'poor' and find with them 'good news' in what John is offering?

---

3   Malachi 4, 5

4   Matthew 3:3

5   Matthew 3:2

For the expectant 'crowd' - tax collectors, soldiers, those with few or no possessions - their question is: 'What should we do now?' John instructs them to let those with two coats give one away - likewise excess food. Tax collectors who frequently supplemented their wages by extortion, he directs - 'Take no more than your due'. Soldiers are told 'No extortion! No intimidation! Be content with your pay!'[6]

Advent's 'shaking reality' is that it is a season of partridge and penance. A time when we expect to give and receive in the name of the coming 'day of the Lord'. John's question to us is: 'What will we "cut away"?' He summons us, says Delp, 'to the opportunity of warding off, by the greater power of the converted heart, the shifting desert that will pounce upon us and bury us.'

Prayer

We hear today the call to prepare, O Lord, for your just and gentle rule to come into our world.

We who have more than one coat, and much spare food, know how so much of what we call 'ours' deprives others of what might be called 'theirs'.

We do not see ourselves as particularly 'holy', or even 'good', but we want to heed the call of John, who baptised all prepared to 'cut away' from privilege and power, and serve you amongst the disenfranchised and powerless. Lord hear us.

---

6   Luke 3:14, NJB

The Third Tuesday
A messenger to construct a way ...

John the Baptist was a desert dweller. Here, amidst its harsh terrain, he had learned to read its signs: the tracks of animals, the direction of wind etched into the dunes, sources of water, the breeding ground of locusts, and the hives of wild honey. Here in the wilderness he found refuge, solitude and his vocation to bring justice to life.[1] In the crude simplicity of a diet of locusts and wild honey, his physical and spiritual hunger was met. In the solitude, hunger for God's saving justice was to be met in the honing of his message of repentance and expectation of the One 'stronger' than himself.

Elijah, too, was a man of the desert. A solitary, not given much to human company, he was witness to a divided and dividing nation. Internecine rivalry had split the nation into two rival kingships of Israel and Judah. In Israel, King Ahab and his wife Jezebel turned to the worship of Baal, the local god of fertility and economic prosperity. Neglecting the core constitutional commandment, 'Thou shalt have no other gods but me', they set out to destroy the prophets of the Lord.

At the instigation of God, Elijah seeks through a series of interventions to restore the nation's faith in God and unite its peoples. A man of zeal and enormous energy, his actions seemed

---

1   Isaiah 32:16

to do nothing but provoke the monarch's anger. Exhausted, disillusioned and depressed, he escaped to a cave in the desert. There God found him and questioned: 'Why are you here, Elijah?' 'Because of my great zeal for the Lord the God of Hosts,' Elijah responded. 'The people of Israel have forsaken your covenant, torn down your altars, and put your prophets to the sword. I alone am left, and they seek to take my life.'[2]

Elijah's spiritual and emotional state concern God. Elijah's sense of defeat, with its accompanying anger and resentment, causes God to decide on a replacement. Elijah is to anoint Elisha as his successor. When the young man asks to be able to say goodbye to his folks, Elijah tells him to 'Go back.' These same words were used by God in relieving Elijah from his prophetic task. Is Elijah, in his defeat, unwilling to engage the one he has anointed in God's name to such a fearsome and demanding task?

By the time of John the Baptist, Elijah carried the stuff of legend on his shoulders, a 'Hero of God's People'. It is his adventures in fighting against corruption, his integrity in upholding the powerless, and his zeal for God that people remember. 'A voice crying in the wilderness' has an element of the poetic about it. The cost, the danger, risk and sacrifice, not to mention the defeat and despair, these are all forgotten. But not by John.

John observes with clear eye and simplicity of language the reality of the system in which God's people are enslaved. He sees how the worship of God and the application of God's laws have been sublimated to political expediency and the ambition of the religious and secular elites. John sees the 'vipers' of God's garden

---

2   1 Kings 19:13–14. The full story of Elijah's actions can be read in 1 Kings 16:29–1 Kings 22.

re-shaping the liberating truth of Isaiah from 'Good news to the poor' to callous oppression and injustice.

John, whose message to the confused majority, the not needed, the 'poor', is received by them as 'good news' leaving them 'all agog', is not so received by the powers. Already the powers are gathering, and John will be arrested for what St Luke describes as criticism of 'all the evil things that Herod had done, adding to them all by shutting up John in prison'.

Throughout his ministry John has been consistent in pointing hearers towards 'one who is more powerful than I.' On the arrest of John, St Mark records, 'Jesus came into Galilee proclaiming the good news of God, and saying, "The time is fulfilled, and the kingdom of God has come near; repent and believe the good news".' It is the same message as that of the now imprisoned John. Just as the mantle of Elijah fell on the shoulders of Elisha, so Jesus now steps up to the plate, confronted by the same challenges, facing the same foes, and committed to the same gospel.

In his prison cell, John faced doubts and questions like those of the exhausted and pursued Elijah. John had prophesied fire and judgment. He was old school in his expectations of God - anger, retribution, punishment. John was confused - where was the cleared 'threshing floor' and the 'unquenchable fire'? Jesus' emphasis on healing and freedom from oppression seemed to John to play down judgment.

For Jesus, the gospel is the same, but its focus is on action that will produce its own judgment on a society itself blind, lame, deaf, dead and poor in its obligations. Jesus will follow John through arrest, trial, imprisonment and execution. His words will speak, but his actions will speak louder. Jesus, John, Elijah, all the 'crying voices', refuse to be suppressed, 'so that', in Alfred Delp's words, 'those who today are our executioners will not tomorrow become accusers because we have remained silent.'

As in the day of Elijah, John and Jesus, our world is divided, cruel and bitter. The crushing power of consumption and affluence, the illusion of security and fear of difference, are hard to escape. The 'shaking reality' of Advent nevertheless calls us to do so by turning towards those who are repressed, distorted and objectified. For when judgment comes - in whatever form it takes - we will not be accused of keeping silent. Just as God sent John to construct the way for Jesus; so Jesus constructs the way for his disciples; and the gospel writers construct the way for us to follow.

A Prayer

Blessed Lord, without you we cannot find the courage
to 'cry out',
Mercifully grant us your Holy Spirit to direct and rule
our hearts,
For the sake of your kingdom, and your glory.

The Third Wednesday
Increase our faith ...

For a dozen or so years, a group of colleagues met for an Advent retreat. A time to reflect on the past year, to take stock and to seek guidance. Our gifted guide would bring us poetry and music, in addition to her own wealth of wisdom and understanding of God's word. During one such retreat in the Cornwall seaside town of Newquay we had been listening to some words from the poet-songwriter Leonard Cohen.

For copyright reasons I cannot reproduce words from Cohen's song 'Show Me the Place',[1] - but suffice it to say the title itself had something of a prayer about it. The song contained imagery and sentiments that matched our mood and desire. It spoke of a sense of being enslaved to a vision, of stones too heavy to move, of suffering , and of the place and moment where God's Word took on humanity.

All of these sentiments were borne out in our experience. Much as we often found joy and satisfaction in our lives and ministries, we, like the poet, experienced times of feeling enslaved, unable to move stones of resistance either in our own lives, or amongst those with whom we ministered. We knew the realities and suffering of

---

1   'Show Me the Place' is a track on Leonard Cohen's 2012 album *Old Ideas* - I confess to not really understanding such copyright restrictions when the use of another's poetry or songs would lead to greater awareness of their work, and presumably increased sales.

busyness, over-tiredness and the frustration of not seeing Christ's way as clearly as we would wish.

The song affected us all in slightly different ways. In the evening we took a little time to tell it as it is. Folk courageously and powerfully voiced concerns as to how much longer we could continue to serve God, when so many apparent imponderables faced us. During the previous year, like the disciples, we had often prayed, 'Lord, increase our faith'. Like the disciples, we seemed to hear a response: 'If you had faith the size of a mustard seed, you could say to this mulberry tree: "Be uprooted, and planted in the sea", and it would obey you.'[2]

By Advent our 'mustard seed' faith was more than a little jaundiced. Like Elijah, we had experienced our share of defeats and anxieties. Yet the words of the Cohen song in which he had reflected a sense of being enslaved to a vision had become something of a prayer for us. Were we somehow 'slaves' of Christ? At times it had felt like it.

Following on Jesus' call for 'mustard seed' faith, he asks his disciples to imagine they were slave owners. Then he asked, how would you treat a slave who had worked all day but was also obliged to prepare his/her owner's meal before taking time for themselves? 'Do you thank the slave for doing what was commanded?' Jesus enquires. Expecting the answer 'No', he concludes: 'So you, also, when you have done all that you were ordered to do, say, 'We are worthless slaves; we have done only what we ought to have done.'[3]

In Jesus' time slavery was institutional, part of the fabric of society. Today human trafficking and child slavery are terrible realities. Contemporary Christian discipleship focuses more on

---

2   Luke 17:5–7

3   Luke 17:7–10

what God can do to protect, comfort and limit our suffering, rather than marking us out as 'slaves of Christ'. It is almost as if roles are reversed, and God is our servant. When we truly seek God's kingdom and its saving justice we should not be surprised that, like Elijah, John and Jesus, there are times when our faith is tested and our vision blurred. We need 'mustard seed' moments.

For Elijah in his cave, John in his prison cell, and Jesus on the Mount of Olives, there was a mustard seed moment that offered just sufficient encouragement to keep on keeping on. For Elijah, it was God's provision of Elisha; for John it was Jesus' - 'Go tell John what you see and hear' speech; and for Jesus himself it was the intimacy of a conversation on the Mount of Transfiguration. [4]

And Delp from the confines of his prison cell - 'three paces this way, and three paces that way' - found comfort in an angel: 'given to me two years ago for Advent by a kind person. The angel bore the inscription, "Rejoice, for the Lord is near". The angel was destroyed by a bomb. A bomb killed the man who gave it to me, and I often feel he is doing me the service of an angel.'

During our retreat we faced up once again to the truth that when God bids us to follow, God bids us to come and die. In an age of the self, of 'me first', such a call is folly. Yet for Elijah, John and Jesus, laying aside all that would detract from the emergence of God's gracious rule in the hearts and lives of humanity opened the door to hope. So it is for us. The story is told of children who asked - 'Where does the Messiah come from?' The narrator replied that he has never been away. He is to be found among the beggars by the pool. He is distinguished from the other beggars. Each of them wears clean clothes. Every day they take their clothes off and wash them, replacing them when they are dried. Except for the

---

4   Matthew 17:1–8

Messiah. He removes his clothes one item at a time to wash, dry and put back on. 'Why?' queried the children. 'Because he wants to be ready to come at any time.' 'And when is that?' - the children asked again. 'Whenever enough people want him to,' replied the story teller.

During our retreat such stories encouraged us. Together we wanted to be shown the places of suffering; we wanted Jesus to tell us where as his slaves we are to go - we also wanted to be able to roll the stone away that barred our heart and soul from welcoming the Word made flesh. Above all we acknowledged that we couldn't do this in our own strength. If Jesus was ready to come at any time - we wanted him now. The 'shaking reality of Advent' is that it is a time to 'increase our faith'. It is a time to look at the grains of mustard seed that could command the trees that block the path to faith, hope and love to be 'uprooted and planted in the sea'. It is time to welcome again the One who has never been away, and 'Rejoice, the Lord is near.' It is time to pray 'show me the place'.

Prayer

Teach us, good Lord, to find in those moments of quiet despair and desperation the mustard seed of faith. And in our times of loneliness to accept that you are ready to come and meet us at any time. But above all, as we seek to welcome you as the Word become human, will you show us the place once more where you want us to serve, for your Kingdom and love's sake.

The Third Thursday
Speaking truth to power

'Speaking truth to power' always carries risks. For many around the world those risks include the very real possibility of arrest, imprisonment, torture and death. It is hard to face up to such realities during a season when there is supposed to be 'peace on earth and goodwill to all'. Yet in this third week of Advent, when our focus is upon John the Baptist as a fore-runner of Jesus, we cannot ignore the cost of that to John.

St Mark tells us that Herod arrested John because of his criticism of an incestuous marriage. Marriages amongst rulers were a matter of politics. It was through them that kings built up their influence and dynasties. Whilst we do not know the details, and it seems like a thin excuse for such an arrest, it is clear that John was a thorn in Herod's side, understanding as he did the incestuous relationship of Herod's government and court. Jesus was to warn his disciples later 'beware of the leaven (or yeast) of Herod'. We may understand the term 'leaven' here to mean the power networks that ensured Herod's security, and continued patronage by the Romans.

What ultimately sealed John's fate, however, was neither a judge's sentence nor the hollow mockery of a show trial: it was a drunken oath made to a dancing girl. John's life was bartered to save royal face. There was a party. Present were the social elite of Galilee. Herod's wife Herodias bore a grudge against John, and sought to have him removed. Herod himself is said to have 'feared John, knowing that he was a righteous and holy man, and he protected him. When he heard him, he was greatly perplexed, and yet he liked to listen to him.'[1]

A dancing girl, widely thought to be Herodias's daughter, delighted the audience. Such dancing was often quite erotic, and usually reserved for family events only. Herod's male guests could hardly believe their eyes, not least because an honourable parent would not permit such a display from a female member of the family. Herod not only 'shamed' the girl, but also 'shamed' the men watching such sensuality.

As the dance concluded, one imagines to whistles and catcalls, drunk or sober, Herod offered all he could to the girl, 'even half my kingdom'. Women at this time were regarded as only worth half a man's worth. Herod could not promise her his whole realm. The oath would have been public. If he were to keep the trust of his officers, he would have to grant whatever the girl asked. Herodias's daughter consulted her mother, who seized the chance of Herod's impulsive oath. Knowing that he dare not lose face in front of the Galilean top brass, she sent the girl back, demanding, 'I want you to give me at once the head of John the Baptist on a platter'.

Herod was trapped. Hoisted, we might say, on his own petard. The power networks he had so studiously built up watched. Weakness now could play into the hands of rivals. A midnight execution, so beloved of despots, was ordered. John's head, which symbolised John's honour, was sacrificed to rescue the king as a consequence of his drunken oath.

---

1   Mark 6:20

'Speaking truth to power' is not something that most of us are encouraged to do in our churches, or our practice of spirituality. Yet all of us, as we look at our society and the world in which we live, and witness injustice, widespread violation of human rights, the destruction of the environment, and the massive divisions between rich and poor, know how power corrupts and destroys humanity.

Though we often talk about the cross, and of Jesus' sacrifice, rarely are we challenged to make a major sacrifice for our faith. Ours is an age of comfortable religion, religion that ensures our spiritual well-being and fitness for eternity. By and large, contemporary Christianity covers up the truly radical Jesus prophesied by John the Baptist. In the West it is not a faith which brings us before the courts to defend our stance against those things that destroy abundant living.

Elsewhere in the world we witness those who suffer harassment, jail, violence, torture and even death, and they rightly become the subject of our prayers. But to what extent does their plight, and those of others suffering from poverty and injustice, lead us to 'speak truth to power'? There is so much wrong and so little appears to change, we reason, what's the point?

Desmond Tutu used to illustrate the problem like this: 'How do you eat an elephant? One bite at a time.' So with 'speaking truth to power'. We pray, and ask God to prompt us to find the courage to speak up for someone, or group that cannot speak for themselves. It might take a 'bite' in the form of a letter, a conversation, joining a group of like-minded people, or taking part in some form of direct action. 'Whatever you do will be insignificant, but it is very important that you do it', said Gandhi, adding a touch of realism, but also of truth.

The 'shaking reality' of Advent reminds us in the story of John the Baptist of the cost of discipleship to the One who is coming. Whatever you do, be assured that God will not demand of you more than you can be given strength to undertake. Neither can you do everything. Life happens. But never doubt that a small group of people committed to change are the only ones who really ever make a difference.

Prayer

Lord of life,
your servant John the Baptist
spoke truth to power to prepare for your coming.
Help us, like John, to work together for that day
when your kingdom comes and justice and mercy
are experienced by all humanity.

The Third Friday
What is keeping you ...?

Speaking to a conference of Christians nearly forty years ago, a Native American said: 'Regardless of what the New Testament says, most Christians are materialists, with no real experience of the Spirit, and most Christians are individualists, with no real commitment to community'. Looking over a group of theologians, clergy and Christian leaders, he continued: 'Let's pretend that you are all Christians. You would not accumulate, you would actually love one another, you would share everything you had with each other and with the poor, and you would treat each other as if you were a family.' He finished with a question: 'What is it that keeps you from doing that?' Not one had a good answer to his question.[1]

This unlikely John the Baptist figure shocked his audience into silence. For me the words tumbled out of an article I had been reading at the time. Sorting through some journals recently, I came across the original with a frayed cover, pages browning at the edges from repeated thumbing through the years, together with untidy underlinings and scribbled margin notes. I was reminded of how these words had shaped my life, but how too they acted as something of a 'shaking reality' on what still remains to be done.

Back in the 1980s there was a certain youthful idealism wrapped up in the vision which somehow the words of the conference

---

1   Adapted from 'Rebuilding the Church' by Jim Wallis, *Sojourners*, January 1980

speaker exemplified. Many Christians tried different forms of communal living; some experimented with sharing economic resources, and many sought to put into practice a faith that does justice. It seemed that people were consciously seeking a base that was internally strong enough to enable us to survive as Christians.

The idea of 'sharing everything', 'treating each other as if ... family', breaking bread, praying[2] and 'making a preferential option for the poor',[3] seemed to crystallise what it meant to be the church. It was a call to love one another and to offer our lives for the sake of the world.

Idealism quickly gave way to the realisation of how difficult and challenging community can be. People bring who they are 'warts and all' to such living. They carry with them their egos, the shared insecurity of the world around, selfishness, prejudice, desire for power, as well as much other 'stuff.' Christian community puts us in touch with our fears, hates, and even the violence within ourselves.

Learning to trust, to disarm from our fears, let go our prejudice, and learn to 'love our enemies' in whatever form they present themselves, is as much a part of what it means to love one another and offer our life for the sake of the world as practising a faith that does justice. 'Love in action is harsh and dreadful when compared to love in dreams,' observed Dorothy Day, who founded the *Catholic Worker*. But who promised it would be otherwise?

Living in community, as the monastic orders have found through the centuries, is far from being a vocation for everyone. Yet if we are to belong to Christ and to each other, what St Paul calls 'being the body of Christ', we have to move beyond our individualism, and one hour on Sundays. The 'shaking reality' of

---

2   Acts 2:42–43

3   The phrase 'preferential option for the poor' emerged from the Second Vatican Council as a key vocation for God's Church.

Advent is that it reminds us that if we are 'to do justly, love mercy and walk with God', as the prophet Micah has it, then it begins with the love and unity of those of us who claim to be a new 'family' in Jesus Christ.

It is not enough to say, 'Don't look at the church, look at Jesus'. From the beginning Jesus built community. They were to be his ongoing, visible presence in the world: living as family, following Jesus' teaching, sharing, breaking bread, praying, and seeking 'the things that make for peace'.[4] Advent reminds us that God's people are called 'out' of the world, 'into' a relationship with one another; and then are 'sent' back by God into the world - to feed the hungry, clothe the naked, house the homeless, heal the sick, and visit the imprisoned.[5]

Advent asks us: 'What is keeping you from doing that?' Alfred Delp says, 'If we want to transform life again ... then the great Advent question for us is whether we come out of these convulsions with this determination: yes, arise! It is time to wake from sleep. It is time for a waking up to begin somewhere. It is time to put things back where God the Lord put them. It is time for each of us to go to work with the same unshakable sureness that the Lord will come to set our life in God's order wherever we can. Where God's word is heard, he will not cheat our life of the message; where our life rebels before our own eyes, he will reprimand it.'

Prayer

Open our eyes to see you, Lord,
open our ears to hear you

---

4   Luke 19:42

5   Matthew 25:31–46

open our hearts to love you
for your kingdom and your truth's sake.

The Third Saturday
Hear the gentle step of announcing angels

On a bright, sunny, summer morning I stood in the cell block at Sachsenhausen concentration camp outside Berlin, where Pastor Martin Niemöller had been incarcerated for four years during the Nazi era. Here in a prison within a prison he witnessed the worst excesses of humanity's inhumanity, through what must have seemed an eternity. I was writing the early reflections of this book at the time, and outside Niemöller's cell, my mind was drawn to Alfred Delp's imprisonment in an environment he described as 'doubly secure'. And my mind and heart were filled with both fear and wonderment.

Fear, because surrounded by 'four walls and the prison walls of our grey days', as Delp described his circumstances, I pondered on the apparent impossibility of sustaining faith. Wonder, because Delp was able to reflect: 'For all its earnestness, Advent is a time of inner security, because it has received a message. Oh, if it ever happens that we forget the message and the promises ... if we can no longer hear the gentle step of announcing angels; if our soul is no longer at once shaken and exalted by their whispered word - then it will be all over with us ... The first thing we must do if we want to be alive is to believe in the golden seed of God that the angels have scattered and still offer to open our hearts.'

During this final week of Advent we shall hear more loudly, and I hope with greater clarity, the voice of Alfred Delp. His witness from the prison cell and martyr's gibbet, three quarters of a century ago, resonates profoundly today. In his meditation, Delp focused much of his attention on 'The Crier in the Wilderness', 'The Angel of the Annunciation', and the 'Blessed Woman'. Whilst we may interpret them as John the Baptist, Gabriel and the Virgin Mary, Delp's intention is that we should perceive them as archetypes upon whom we can model our own witness.

During the past few days 'The Crier in the Wilderness' has warned us both of 'The devastation (that) will soon be so terrifying and universal that the word "wilderness" will again strike our hearts and minds …'. But also of '…the great comfort known only to those who have paced out the inmost and furthermost boundaries of existence'.

Tomorrow, on Advent's Fourth Sunday, the candle will be lit symbolising Mary, the 'Blessed Woman'. She, like John the Baptist, Alfred Delp, Martin Niemöller, Etty Hillesum and countless others, knew both the blessing of intimacy with God, and the devastation of the 'sword' that pierces body and soul.[1]

In one of his BBC 'Thought for the Day' broadcasts, Rabbi Jonathan Sacks spoke of living in a time of unprecedented change. He reflected that in such circumstances, the people who survived were neither the strongest nor the fittest, but those who best adapted to change. Of the Jews, he said three things kept them going, despite never knowing where the next persecution or removal would come from:

---

1   Luke 2:35

- to remember 'who they were' - their ancestors, their stories and their community;
- to maintain the hope that despite everything God is with us, however distant He may appear;
- to hold on to the goal of building a world of compassion, love and peace.

These three principles provide something of that 'inner security' of which Advent speaks. They provide, too, a certain 'earnestness', the application of emotional intelligence to the unprecedented time of change upon which Sacks reflects, and the danger of the universal 'wilderness' that Delp predicted.

Advent calls us to 'remember who we are'. To recall the 'message' that has attracted, called and sustained us: the message from a God who announces through his messengers the coming of a time of peace and justice. Advent calls us to maintain hope in God, even when evil appears to triumph everywhere, and the gates of heaven seem deaf to our cries. Far from allowing us to languish in the waiting room for the kingdom to come, Advent bids us open our eyes, minds and hearts to the possibilities of building a world of compassion, love and peace.

All of those whose stories have been told thus far in the journey towards Christmas have been ordinary people, who in times of unprecedented change have found grace to undertake extraordinary things. In this final week, our vision focuses upon Mary. A Galilean woman in the midst of marriage preparation in Nazareth is called to do something extraordinary by God's grace.

Mary's story is every prophet's story, and it is potentially our story too. Like Mary, John the Baptist, Alfred Delp and Etty Hillesum, the tasks that they faced seemed beyond their own abilities. But, as so often in times when God seems most absent,

God is revealed in the courage, faith and obedience of faithful, listening people. The prophet who says 'yes' takes great risk. He or she knows that being singled out for God's favour will take their very being, and they will need accompaniment and grace to see it through. The 'shaking reality' of Advent this week is once again 'to believe in the golden seed of God that the angels have scattered and still offer to open our hearts.'

Prayer

Lord
in these times of unprecedented change,
your angels still scatter the golden seed of your promises,
and challenge us to still offer to open our hearts.
Help us to remember from Whom and where we come,
that despite everything, you are with us.
Give us, as you gave to Mary and all the prophets and saints
through the generations, grace to work towards the goal
of a world of compassion, justice, love and peace,
through Jesus Christ our Saviour.

The Fourth Sunday
Rejoice … favoured one

This week begins with angels. 'These are not yet the loud angels of rejoicing that come out into the open, the angels of Advent,' says Alfred Delp. 'Quiet, inconspicuous, they come into rooms and before hearts as they did then. Quietly they bring God's questions and proclaim to us the wonders of God, for whom nothing is impossible.'

Angels call us to believe, reports Alfred Delp. For most of us, angels form the stuff of the Christmas and Easter stories, but in our materialistic, scientific age, few of us would claim to have encountered such beings. Or is it that we have, but not recognised them as such? Part of the problem is presentation. Is it maybe the 'wings and things' that popular artistic presentation offers us that blinds our eyes and spirits to *ho angelos* - God's 'messengers'?

Bath Abbey, one of the most beautiful churches in England, was given a series of angel marquettes that adorn the choir stalls. They provided the opportunity for the church's publicity team to describe the Abbey as a place 'where earth and heaven meet'. To my mind this is the role and function of angels, to provide a meeting place between the human and the divine.

The gospel writers make no attempt to describe the appearance of 'God's messengers', the angels: they simply tell us of how they encounter individuals in the midst of their daily tasks and duties. Each who is visited expresses surprise at being the subject of God's attention. Yet each, with the possible exception of Zechariah,[1] does not believe what they are told and accept the message as 'God given'.

Ours is an age that does not manage easily with mystery. Yet the most casual glance at the plethora of television programmes about our knowledge of the universe, or even our own planet, exposes us all the time to wonder and mystery. A few days before these lines were written the spacecraft that has sought to reveal the secrets of Saturn and its moons for a dozen years has left us with more questions than answers, as well as causing us to re-think previous knowledge. And in 2017 BBC's *Blue Planet 2* attracted the largest television audience of the year.

For many years a friend, who could often be quite inconvenient in both his surprise visits and dietary requirements, nevertheless had the capacity to somehow always bring a word of truth, hope and inspiration. I called him my 'angel'. At times, like the glass angel that tinkles annoyingly against the window of my prayer space on windy days, his message was insistent, but always redemptive. Courage would be strengthened, despair dispelled and consolation brought, and a 'word from the Lord' always given.

My 'angel' was not a comfortable figure. His persona was at times abrupt, direct and uncompromising. Far from the white-satined apparition with half-bent wings sticking from shoulder blades that the school nativity so often represents, he was often mistaken for a tramp. As now, so then the appearance of an angel did not immediately presage 'good news'. Gabriel, the war angel in Jewish tradition, appeared to both Zechariah and Mary. Zechariah's

---

1   Luke 1:5–21. Zechariah questioned the angel Gabriel over the biological impossibility of conceiving a child because he and his wife were 'getting on in years'

response was one of terror, prompting Gabriel to say: 'Do not be afraid.'

To Mary, Gabriel offers a greeting unique in Scripture: 'Rejoice, favoured one.'[2] Most translations record Mary as being 'perplexed' at receiving such a greeting. In Greek the word is *charitoō*, from the root word *charis* - meaning 'kindness', 'grace'. But the message the angel brings is one that has an undercurrent of threat, terror and scandal. As a young woman she knows all too well the stigma of being an unmarried mother. Not only that, but the disregard with which the occupying forces regarded Jewish women meant that she could be perceived as being a victim of rape at worst, or collaboration at best.

When Mary has grasped what the angel proposes, at least in the matter of being a mother, Gabriel seeks to reassure her, not only that 'nothing is impossible for God', but that 'the Holy Spirit will over shadow you, and the power of the Most High will over shadow you'. Whilst undoubtedly such remarks are designed to explain the activity of God in the child's conception, we must also read them as indicators of God's protection, and the assurance of safe deliverance.

Like the prophet Isaiah, who proclaimed that the 'Spirit of the Lord is upon me,'[3] so Mary experiences God's power come upon her. In response she freely gives her consent, and receives the Spirit. With all the practicality of womanhood, Mary knows she will need human accompaniment through this exciting and perilous time. She journeys to the hill country and the home of her cousin Elizabeth. Greeting Elizabeth in the language of the angel, she repeats the news of God's favour. Like the angel, Mary reaches

---

2   Luke 1:26–38

3   Isaiah 61:1

out to the aged Elizabeth in support, love and grace. 'Earth and heaven meet' in the simplicity of a village home.

The 'shaking reality' of Advent invites us to become recipients of God's grace and kindness. We are called to listen to the angels who, 'Quiet, inconspicuous … come into rooms and before hearts as they did then. Quietly they bring God's question and proclaim the wonders of God, for whom nothing is impossible'. Our 'angels' may be very human, even irritatingly insistent, but what they bring is the persistent hope of a 'new order of things, of life, of our existence'. We light the final purple candle to remind us of Mary's call to bear the Christ child, and of ours too.

Prayer

Lord,
you sent your messenger Gabriel
to speak words of grace and truth to your servant Mary.
Grant to us, whom you also bless with your favour,
to respond with open hearts to those who need our support
and presence, to remind and encourage them of the truth,
'nothing will be impossible with God'.

The Fourth Monday
Womb compassion

There is something beautifully moving about the encounter between Elizabeth and Mary in the Judean hill town. St Luke records the moment between these women of courage and peace: 'When Elizabeth heard Mary's greeting, the child leaped in her womb. And Elizabeth was filled with the Holy Spirit and exclaimed with a loud cry, 'Blessed are you among women, and blessed is the fruit of your womb. And why has this happened to me? For as soon as I heard the greeting, the child in my womb leaped for joy ....'[1]

This gesture of solidarity between the two women is expressed in the very physical moment of the nascent John the Baptist's 'quickening'. Elizabeth experiences a double joy. She, whom her husband described to the angel as 'getting on in years',[2] and who describes herself as experiencing 'disgrace I have endured among my people'[3], is now a mother-to-be. After the seclusion and isolation of the first months of her confinement, she is now joined by Mary, whom she names, 'the mother of my Lord'.

Both women have borne the stigma of public shame and disgrace. As Mary's pregnancy became evident she would have been subject to questioning gossip in the tight-knit village

---

1   Luke 1:41–44

2   Luke 1:18

3   Luke 1.25

community. 'Was she seduced, or raped?' Her betrothed, Joseph, was known as a 'righteous man',[4] so if he wasn't the father, then did she choose someone else? Unlikely and unpalatable as such questions might be to us, who have the benefit of hindsight with stories of angels and annunciations, such would have seemed something of an idle tale in the village.

The calumny experienced by both women was counter-balanced as 'filled with the Holy Spirit', they celebrated together their participation in the fulfilment of God's promise. A promise to restore and remake humanity, where the old divisions and ways of the powerful over the weak will be swept away, and all have equal place. And it will be accomplished through the womb of a woman. Elizabeth will bear John, 'who will make ready a people prepared for the Lord',[5] Mary will bear the one who will be called 'Jesus, for he will save his people from their sins', and become 'God with us'.[6]

Hebrew is a language that often describes emotions in pictures. One description of God's grace is 'womb compassion'; and God's compassion as 'the movement of the womb of God'.[7] God's pain is associated with that of the menstrual cycle, and giving birth. When Moses and God wrestled over what to do about the fickleness of the Israelites during their journey from captivity in Egypt to freedom in the Promised Land, God reveals 'womb compassion' for the people. [8]

Such a description both shocks and surprises, revealing as it does not only an intimate association with the feminine, but of a

---

4   Matthew 1:19

5   Luke 1:17

6   Matthew 1:21, 23

7   The Hebrew word is *rahamim*

8   Exodus 34:6

depth of suffering and longing that goes beyond our expectation. One writer, Martha Nussbaum, has described such compassion as 'a painful emotion directed at the serious suffering of another creature or creatures'. And it is only compassion of such an order that can overcome what she calls the 'othering of others'.[9]

In the outburst of the *Magnificat*, Mary's song, the 'movement of the womb of God' is evidenced by its focus on the rescue of lives damaged by injustice, power, greed and shame. These are those whom St Luke later refers to as 'the little ones', or 'those who cringe'[10] - or as we might say, 'them others'.

In 2013 Pope Francis visited the Mediterranean island of Lampedusa, where countless refugees had landed in their bid to escape war, persecution and poverty. In his speech he reminded his hearers of the danger of losing our moral sense, our compassion, and the ease with which we 'other others' whom we perceive to be different from ourselves. The Pope spoke of the indifference of our times towards the world's 'little ones' and of the attendant dangers of such neglect.

The Pope asked his hearers to remember God's question to Cain, the brother of Abel, whom he had slain: 'Where is your brother?' Cain represented the resistance to compassion, the loss of morality, the inability to weep for the 'other'. Then in the light of the thousands of refugees who had drowned in the Mediterranean, Pope Francis asked, 'Who among us has wept for these things, and things like this?' He added, 'We are a society that has forgotten the experience of "weeping with". The globalisation of indifference has taken from us the inability to weep!'

---

9   Martha C. Nussbaum, *Political Emotions - Why Love Matters for Justice* (Belknapp, Harvard, 2013)

10 St Luke uses the word *anawim* which encompasses those who lack justice and liberty

The 'shaking reality' of Advent is that it reminds us there is compassion in God's judgment. God is not indifferent towards injustice. Judgment must come. The God whose 'womb compassion' cries out against all that is unjust and de-humanising nevertheless offers mercy, forgiveness and the gift of beginning again to nations, communities and individuals who come to believe 'another world is possible'.[11] Such news causes children 'to leap in the womb', and fills beings with the Holy Spirit.

Prayer

Lord, who out of stigma and shame brought your servants Mary and Elizabeth,
causing them to believe 'another world is possible',
so move us to a womb compassion like Yours,
that we do not just remember how to weep over indifference in our world,
but strive for a justice that restores to all true equality as your daughters and sons,
that the world may believe the Coming One is true Messiah.

---

11 'Another world is possible' is the motto of the World Social Forum.

The Fourth Tuesday
Mary's song

Evensong is said to be amongst the most widely attended acts of worship. It is sung daily in Cathedrals, and in the United Kingdom is broadcast on BBC radio. Amongst those who attend, or listen, are undoubtedly devout people of faith, but it is surprising how many people become what the atheist philosopher Richard Dawkins described as 'cultural Anglicans', allowing the musical settings, and cadences of psalms and canticles, to provide a measure of 'soul food'.

From time to time I have been asked to speak in university chapels at Sunday evensong. Almost always I have reflected on the radical nature of the canticles the *Magnificat* and the *Nunc Dimittis*,[1] which are set for this Daily Office. Given the political and religious turmoil out of which the Book of Common Prayer emerged in 1662, and the role of the Crown and State, it is hard to imagine how the *Magnificat,* in particular, passed the censor!

The *Magnificat* - 'Mary's song' - is sung by the 'Blessed Woman' - as Alfred Delp calls her, after her journey to the hill country to accompany Elizabeth in her confinement. The women 'bless' each other. The concept of the 'blessed woman' lay deep in Jewish

---

1   The *Magnificat* - Mary's song: Luke 1:46–55: *Nunc Dimittis* - Simeon's song Luke 2:26-32.

history. Two women in particular bear this title: Jael and Judith.[2] Both have songs of praise written about them, though it is likely that Judith is an apocryphal character. Both, too, were praised for their heroic nationalism, and noted for their violence. Both were seen as preparing for the coming of God's kingdom.

Some scholars believe that the origins of 'Mary's song' - *Magnificat* - are to be found in Maccabean war hymns. Be that as it may, Mary and Elizabeth are described as being 'filled with Holy Spirit' and they prophesy. Elizabeth acknowledges Mary as the mother-to-be of 'My Lord', and Mary is inspired to prophesy the coming of a radical new order.

Mary speaks first of how God has favoured a humble peasant woman. The sub-text of such a revelation in an age when male priests were seen to be the sole conduit of divine grace was obvious, and profoundly subversive. If God's purpose could be fulfilled by God becoming a mother's son, then, as Delp understood it, 'The world has come under a different law ... Advent is the promise denoting the new order of things, of life, of our existence.'

It is from Mary's lips that St Luke prepares us for the coming of a new order. Here also, those who have been made poor and hungry are 'lifted up' and 'filled with good things'. Here also, those who have profited from injustice, exploitation and oppression are 'brought down' and 'sent empty away'. This is not a matter of reversing roles. It is 'God's justice ... creating a circle in which all have an equal place at the table, all are in right relation, each one knowing their integrity and preciousness in God's eyes, each one

---

2 Jael in The Book of Judges 5:24–27; Judith in The Book of Judith 13:18 (in the Apocrypha).

free to love fully.'³ 'Not only is 'another world possible', observed the Jesuit martyr Ignaçio Ellacuria, 'another world is necessary.'

Achieving such a 'necessary' world requires two 'simultaneous movements: the empowerment of those formerly oppressed, and relinquishment on the part of those holding the power, the privilege and status.'⁴

When Delp writes from his prison cell that Mary 'is the most comforting of all the Advent figures', we must not allow ourselves to sentimentalise such 'comfort'. The *Magnificat* ain't no sweet lullaby. During the British Raj in India, the *Magnificat* was banned in worship for fear of its revolutionary potential. As recently as the 1980s its public recitation was banned for the same reason in Guatemala.

A friend of mine who attended Sung Evensong most days used to observe that he sat and let the music and liturgy 'wash over him'. His work was hard and demanding, and the contemplative nature of the office provided him with the means of re-charging his spiritual batteries. He was a man of immense prophetic vision, deeply committed to the ecological well-being of the planet and animal welfare; I have no doubt that Mary's words acted as inspiration.

Rightfully comforting though such liturgy can be, contemporary religion, in its desire to be accessible, also risks taking the edge off the radical demands of God's new order. Perhaps in the very beauty of the music and settings of the *Magnificat*, for example, there is a danger of being lulled into a false sense of well-being.

---

3   *New Perspectives on the Nativity* edited by Jeremy Corley (T & T Clark, 2009), Barbara E. Reid, p.40

4   Ibid.

The *Magnificat* has revolutionary potential, as I remind student congregations. Its 'shaking reality' is that it both inspires and calls us to wait actively as Mary did, for the 'Coming One'. Because, as Delp reminds us: 'So many need their courage strengthened, so many are in despair and in need of consolation, there is so much harshness that needs a gentle hand and an illuminating word of release, so much loss and pain in search of inner meaning'. He concludes that we as 'God's messengers know of the blessing that the Lord has cast like seed into these hours of history'.

Prayer

My soul magnifies the Lord,
and my spirit rejoices in God my Saviour,
for he has looked with favour on the lowliness of his servant.
Surely, from now on all generations will call me blessed:
for the Mighty One has done great things for me, for holy is his name.
His mercy is for those who fear him from generation to generation.
He has shown strength with his arm:
he has scattered the proud in the thoughts of their hearts.
He has brought down the powerful from their thrones,
and lifted up the lowly;
he has filled the hungry with good things, and sent the rich away empty.
He has helped his servant Israel, in remembrance of his mercy, according to the promise he made to our ancestors, to Abraham and his descendants for ever.

Luke 1:46-55 NRSV

The Fourth Wednesday
Who do you think you are?

Who Do You Think You Are? has been a popular BBC television programme in which different celebrities have been given the opportunity to pursue enquiries into the history of their family. The outcomes of research frequently surprise, often move, always interest, and occasionally shock. One of the reasons for the programme's appeal is a certain innate curiosity in nearly all of us to find out 'who we are' and 'where we come from'.

Had Mary, the mother of Jesus, been an invitee to consider the question 'Who do you think you are?', she would undoubtedly have been surprised, moved, and in all probability shocked at the revelations concealed in her family history. If she had turned to St Matthew for elements of her story, she would have found a genealogy that included male ancestors, including Abraham and King David, as well as a line of lesser-known characters.

All that would have seemed fairly normal, predictable even. What would have interested, possibly surprised, and even shocked Mary, was to discover that Matthew had included in the list of her ancestors, four women, five - if she included herself.[1] Given that genealogies in the Middle East are recorded exclusively through the male line, the inclusion of women would have been a cause of surprise.

---

1   Matthew 1:1-17

The shock factor for Mary might well have been experienced in the names of the women in her husband-to-be Joseph's line. They were: Tamar, Rahab, Ruth, and Bathsheba. To each of these women was attached a measure of scandal or detriment. For Mary, too, there was the issue of the unconventional pregnancy, always the source of gossip and speculation for a single mother in a close village society.

Neither Tamar, Rahab, Ruth nor Bathsheba fitted comfortably into a Jewish lineage. *Tamar* was a Canaanite woman who had been betrayed by her brother-in-law. She disguised herself, and her father-in-law, Judah, took her for a temple prostitute and had sex with her. Prior to their conjugation, Tamar asked for a pledge and Judah handed her a signet ring, a cord and staff. Months later when she was publicly humiliated for 'playing the whore' and sentenced to be burned, she produced the pledge, exposing Judah as her assailant.[2]

Rahab was also a Canaanite. A prostitute in Jericho, she was visited by two Hebrew spies seeking for the weak points in the city's defences, prior to an intended attack. They stayed the night - presumably as clients. Their whereabouts were discovered, and Rahab faced a demand to deliver them up to the king of Jericho. Admitting they had been clients, Rahab dissembled over who they were and hid the men, arranging their escape after dark by means of ropes hung from her window in the city wall.[3]

Ruth's story is one of the most beautiful and perceptive tales in the Bible. It reveals the humanity of a woman who would have

---

2   Genesis 38

3   Joshua 2

been regarded as an outsider by the Jewish community, and yet became an ancestor both of King David, and Jesus.[4]

Bathsheba was the wife of one of King David's commanders, Uriah. David seduced Bathsheba, and she became pregnant with the child that would one day be King Solomon. To cover his crime, David had Uriah killed.[5]

This ensemble of women, including Mary herself, have stories that are moving, as well as at times shocking and revealing. Common to them all is the truth that God's love and purposes know no boundaries, regardless of the aspirations of individuals and nations to consider themselves to be 'God's favourites' or 'Chosen Ones'. The inclusion of the women is an indication, too, of the failure of patriarchs and monarchs to keep the covenant, assuring them of God's grace and guidance. Matthew, by beginning his gospel with this genealogy, not only follows a tradition of storytelling amongst Middle Eastern people, but announces the arrival, in Jesus, of the era of salvation.

The 'shaking reality' of Advent is that it reveals for us a God whose concern is the welfare and salvation of all people. Matthew's genealogy reveals a pretty rum bunch of men in the ancestry of Jesus. Whilst human nature seeks to distinguish one from another, placing one social, religious, ethnic, gender or national group in a place of superiority to others, God does not. Because all humanity has the propensity to sin, God is not above using for his purposes those who have been either discriminated against, or victimised by others to achieve a wider purpose - the salvation of all.

Thus, in Mary's 'Who do you think you are?' Tamar, Rahab, Ruth, Bathsheba - and indeed Mary herself - remind us not only

---

4 The Book of Ruth

5 2 Samuel 11, 12

of our common humanity, but of the dangers of judging others, and seeking to exclude them from God's grace.

Prayer

Lord,
your word cautions us not to think of ourselves
more highly than we ought;
yet we do so whenever we consider
 our status, gender, ethnicity or nationality
to be more worthy of your love and grace
than others.
Grant us grace, humility, wisdom and love,
so that we may see all, regardless of virtue or vice,
as your beloved.

The Fourth Thursday
The vengeance of God

A persistent little girl was badgering her parents to allow her to be alone with her newborn baby brother. Putting aside their fears that the child might harm the infant, they eventually allowed her her wish. Quietly listening at the door, they heard the baby's sister whisper to her sleeping brother lying in his crib: 'Baby, baby. Tell me what God feels like, I am beginning to forget.'

The prophets, the angels, and Mary, are amongst those who have a profound sense of what God 'feels like'. This is a God who 'brings down the mighty from their seat' and 'lifts up the humble and meek': a God who does not destroy one at the expense of the other, but who seeks to bring both to a recognition of their common humanity, and their status as bearers of God's image. This is the 'veil surrounding all peoples' that needs to be destroyed.

In the next couple of days we shall be celebrating Christmas once again. This Advent will be drawing to a close; a time in which once again we have recalled the Christ who *has come* into the world as Lord and Saviour. It has been a time to remind ourselves of the Christ who *is come*, revealed in the lives of those who seek to follow him. But it is also a time when we anticipate the God who *will come again,* as judge and vindicator. Quite how, and when, remain questions Jesus warned against asking.

What we do know is what the God who *will come again* 'feels like'. Two passages in the New Testament help us here: the first in

Matthew's gospel,[1] where all 'the nations will be gathered before Jesus'. They will be judged on the ways in which they have treated the hungry, thirsty, strangers, sick and imprisoned. Here God is revealed in Jesus as compassionate, and passionate about true justice.

In the second passage in the Book of Revelation,[2] God is shown as making a 'home among mortals'. God will 'wipe away every tear' and remove all indignities that lead to crying, mourning and death. Again we are presented with a God who is compassionate and seeks the welfare of all those who have been victims of loss and death. Again, too, in a poetic way, we are given a picture of the bringing to an end of all that has corrupted and destroyed humanity.

In today's soft-focus faith, where too often sentimentality displaces love, and self-interest displaces true justice, we find surprisingly little talk of judgment. Part of the reason for this lies in our all too human approach to dealing with wrong-doing and those things we perceive as evil in our world, where governments and individuals rarely rise above 'an eye for an eye and a tooth for a tooth', as a response.

Some years ago I heard the story of a small tribal group living in a remote part of Africa. Their society was well ordered, elders were elected to both lead and keep peace amongst their peoples. In the event of a crime or misdemeanour, all work would cease in the village. The elders would call the whole community together. The accused would be arraigned before the people, and the elders would call upon each in turn to speak only good about the one on trial. Sometimes such testimony lasted a few hours, sometimes

---

1   Matthew 25:31–46

2   Revelation 21:1–8, from which all the subsequent references in this section are taken

a few days. Once complete, the senior elder would turn to the accused, and say, 'So how could you, given how well people think of you, behave in such a way?' The sentence had been passed. Shame, and desire to live up to the expectations of the community, the 'punishment'.

Of course it is not a perfect illustration. Sitting in church a while ago, I found myself thinking, I am looking forward to judgment. It was not a thought I had ever had before. Quite what prompted it, I don't know, but three insights emerged from it that helped me. The first was that after many years of Ignatian spiritual practice, I had finally become aware deep within myself that God loved me. And if God loved me, then God must indeed love all humanity.

The second thought was that, given that God has created and loved all that is made, the judgment of God and God's 'vengeance' are the very antithesis of human judgment and vengeance. God's is a judgment of apocalypse - a word that means 'to reveal'. God judges by revealing all that is known of truth, mercy, grace and love. Its power lies in its capacity to cause humanity to shudder at what it has done to its divine Gift.

My third thought was that I should welcome judgment as a disciple of Christ. Why? Because however much I might have tried to follow Christ, I have constantly failed to do so. And because God in Christ seeks to make us whole, fully integrated human beings, self-giving in love to God and humanity, there remains, and will continue to remain much still to be done. Imagine, I wondered, if the compassionate, passionate God who *is to come* enabled me, through that moment of judgment in love, mercy, grace and truth, to come to my senses; could I continue to refuse to love God completely?

In the Christian Orthodox tradition, the day before Easter is referred to as the 'Great Saturday'. During it, believers celebrate the tradition of Christ's 'harrowing of hell'. This commemorates the belief that following his crucifixion Jesus visited the departed souls in Hades, or hell. By his presence he 'harrowed', or turned over the ground of the souls of those present. By so doing, he exposed the truth that there is nowhere that God is not present. And in the light of that, revealed the ever-present possibility of new life. What follows on Easter Day is the celebration of the resurrection, representing the final triumph of God over all things, good and evil.

The 'shaking reality' of Advent lies in the promise of the one who says: 'Surely I am coming soon.' To which, if we truly seek to celebrate Christ's birth, life, death and resurrection, we can only respond: 'Amen. Come Lord Jesus!'[3]

Prayer

Lord, help us to welcome your coming again in judgment; to know that your vengeance is the very antithesis of our understanding, and that you judge by revealing; showing the true power of truth, mercy, love and grace.

You are the God who has never desired the death of sinners, but rather that they should turn from their wickedness and live. May we see that the only 'hell' will be our refusal to accept the awesome reality of your generosity and grace, in this world and the next.

---

3   Revelation 22:20

The Fourth Friday
'For a child has been born for us'

Preparing for Christmas in our parish began in mid-October. A team of people would gather at the Vicarage with the sole purpose of seeking to ensure that whoever entered the church over the Christmas season would be warmly welcomed, and leave enriched and hopeful. The tradition of Nine Lessons and Carols had been quietly ditched in favour of telling the story in a way we hoped would inspire and cause folks to wonder.

Our church was blessed with a sanctuary around which the congregation could sit on three sides. It made for a certain intimacy in what was something of a barn of a building. The altar could be moved on occasion, and our Christmas Carol service was one such. Here, in this space, the drama of the Christmas narrative would be revealed.

Each year was different, and it was always exciting to see what would emerge out of the mix. Our watchwords as we prepared were reverence, rejoicing and revelation. However imaginative, personally committed, and even excited we were about the emerging liturgy, what we sought was the glory of God, and the deepening of faith and love for God.

One year remains a particular memory. As the congregation arrived, the church was partially lit, spotlights focused on the freshly created banners and mobiles hanging from the rafters, telling the familiar stories of angels, shepherds, a stable, manger, a holy family and magi.

At the appointed hour of the service lights were dimmed, the church darkened, and an expectant silence hushed the gathered congregation. Then the sound of rumbling and squeaking army tanks, the noise of loud gunfire, together with the increasing crescendo of the London Symphony Orchestra's recording of *War Child* filled the church.

From out of the darkness and the deafening sounds of warfare came Mary carrying the Christ child, accompanied by Joseph. The sentient words of the prophet Isaiah accompanied their progress:

> *The people who walked in darkness have seen a great light;*
> *those who lived in a land of deep darkness -*
> *on them has the light shined …*

Then a strong, clear youthful voice declared:

> *For a child has been born for us,*
> *a son given to us,*
> *authority rests upon his shoulders*
> *and he is named*
> *Wonderful Counsellor, Mighty God,*
> *Everlasting Father, Prince of Peace.*

A further crescendo in the music grew as a baritone voice declared:

> *His authority shall grow continually,*
> *and there shall be endless peace …*

The music softened a penultimate time -

> *for the throne of David and his kingdom.*
> *He will establish and uphold it*

with justice and righteousness from this time onwards and for ever more.

Through the brightly lit sanctuary the 'Holy Family' passed, a wistful coil of unspoken questions following them: how can a little child 'establish and uphold justice and righteousness', and bring 'endless peace?' The sanctuary empty once more, notes of a carol   beckoned from the organ. The congregation stood to sing the first two verses. Unobtrusively, as the third verse began, a lone actor moved toward the empty sanctuary:

> *But with the woes of sin and strife*
> *the world has suffered long.*
> *Beneath the angel hymns have rolled*
> *two thousand years of wrong,*
> *as warring armies clash and drown.*
> *the love song which they bring:*
> *O hush the noise of bomb and gun*
> *and hear the angels sing.*

Taking a couple of graceful turns, a young man briefly unfurled a 'Ban the Bomb' banner - and as the fourth verse began gathered it up again and returned to his seat. It was not a scripted act.

Like others I had been taken by surprise. In the remaining verse my mind went into over-drive. Some people knew of my convictions concerning matters of war and conflict; would they think this was a set-up? In those brief nano-seconds that the mind takes to decide what to do or say, I concluded it was wisest to say nothing.

Edmund Sears' poem was written in the aftermath of the 1845-48 Mexican American War. Slavery in the United States was a hot topic, as indeed were issues of child labour and the exploitation of the poor. Sears was a man with a social conscience. His poem acted as one of the many 'prompts' to the Christian community to campaign and work for the end of slavery, child labour and poverty.

Our carefully-choreographed opening had been shaken by an unexpected intrusion. Brief, barely discernible, many in the congregation missed it altogether. Yet as Alfred Delp reminds us, Advent brings us a 'message that shakes - so that in the end the world shall be shaken'. He asks: 'How many things have we become used to in the course of the years, of the weeks and months, so that we stand unchecked, unstirred, inwardly unmoved?'

The 'shaking reality' of Advent is that 'Peace on earth, good will to all' is not simply a Christmas mantra, indulged in for a few brief hours of the year. It is the promise of God to the world, given in Christ as Prince of Peace. Just as Christians engaged with bringing an end to slavery, child labour, and many other social ills; so both the prophet and the protestor suggest that war too must disappear from history. Isaiah envisioned such when he declared:

> *all the boots of the tramping warriors*
> *and all the garments rolled in blood*
> *shall be burned as fuel for the fire.*
> *For a child has been born for us*

Prayer

Lord,
as we prepare for your coming among us,
to celebrate the feast of your Son's birth,
help us to be willing to be shaken up.
Where life is firm, may we sense its firmness;
and where it is unstable, uncertain
and without basis or foundation,
enable us to know this too, and endure it.

Christmas Eve
Surprise gifts

> *When peaceful silence lay over all,*
> *and night had run half of her swift course,*
> *down from the heavens , from the royal throne,*
> *leapt your all powerful Word*
> *into the heart of a doomed land the stern warrior leapt.*[1]

Each Christmas Eve these words from the Book of Wisdom encapsulate something of the power of the irruption of God into the human story. Through the years, as I witness crowds entering into abbeys, cathedrals and churches to celebrate God becoming a mother's son, I am unfailingly moved. When the homily has been given, the bread and wine consecrated, I watch and wait. It is the silent beauty of vulnerability revealed in assorted human beings, humbly processing to receive the Body and Blood of Christ, that never fails to touch me.

For a nano-second in the midst of unclear motives, fragile faith and wondering questions, the 'all powerful Word' leaps into hearts and lives, with an 'irruption that smells of stable'.[2] Here, amidst the shaking reality of a God who is in the manger, the wafer pressed into waiting hands, 'the Body of Christ' once borne

---

1   Wisdom 18:14–16, Jerusalem Bible

2   Gustavo Gutiérrez, *The God of Life*, quoted in *Watch for the Light: Readings for Advent and Christmas* (Plough Publishing, 2014) p. 252

by Mary touches tongues with the potential of transforming our world once again.

Here in a cosmic moment both depth and poverty of faith meet. Somehow, we are transformed into something bigger than all our dogmas and differences, all our diversities and disagreements, certainties and uncertainties. Fleetingly the kingdom of God has come on earth as it is in heaven: 'into the heart of a doomed land the stern warrior leapt', bringing hope of new beginnings through God, who speaks to us in a son.

As a child, the excitement of Christmas lay in both the hoped-for and the unexpected gift. Rarely does a Christmas night pass without something of that same sense of expectation and fulfilment. A friend of mine whose son had married a Hindu woman invited her family for Christmas. My friend explained that as a family they would be in church on Christmas night, but that they should feel no obligation to come. 'Oh!' replied the mother, 'we would love to come and meet your God.'

Some years ago I preached and celebrated Holy Communion in Bath Abbey on Christmas night. It had been a time of tension, following a number of terror incidents across European cities, including Britain. Muslim communities were feeling the pressure and vulnerable. In my homily I made a reference to the honour in which Mary was held in Islam. I told of how many Muslims venerate her as a role model, as one who gave herself completely to God. I recalled the tradition of giving Muslim women three dates to eat when they give birth to a child, because it was believed that such fruit was given to Mary upon the birth of Jesus. I ventured that there was much that Christians and Muslims did not agree about the nature of Jesus. I suggested, however, we could find common ground through seeing Mary as one who received God's message and in faith submitted herself to God's will. I questioned, maybe she could be a sign for us all?

Later, as I stood outside the abbey on Christmas morning, I was surrounded by a group of four or five young Pakistani Muslim men and an English man, who told me he was their host. The young men wanted to shake my hand. They had attended the service. Their host told me that it had not been his intention to come; though he was a nominal Christian (as he described himself) it had been his Muslim friends who had wanted to come to honour Jesus, and to revere his mother.

Unexpected Christmas gifts usually surprise us. Sometimes they disappoint. Some are unwanted and are returned or discarded. Some challenge us in the process of receiving them. In an age when religion is perceived by many as the source of conflict, such gifts as those my friend received from her Hindu relatives, and I received from the Muslim men in the Abbey, open our eyes to the universalism of the message of the angels on the Bethlehem hillside: 'Glory to God in the highest heaven and on earth peace among those whom he favours!'

There is a legend from India of a prince, Josaphat, who persecuted Christians. A prophet told him that one day he would become a Christian, and in due course he did. Selling his wealth, renouncing his throne, he pursued his search for truth. The story, however, is something of a legend. It began not as a Christian story, but an Islamic tale. But it does not end there. The story found its roots in the tale of a Hindu prince, who eventually became known as the Buddha. The story passed through many languages and cultures including Arabic, Greek and Latin. The surprise of this story is that 'by a curious route the Buddha became a Christian saint who inspired later generations of Christians (including the Russian novelist Leo Tolstoy) to pursue the path of enlightenment.'[3]

'We may ask,' said Delp, 'why God has sent us into this time' - a time of fear, suspicion, conflict and insecurity. If we perceive this as a question for us to ask ourselves this Christmas Eve, the 'shaking reality' lies in the answer that God has sent us to bear witness, and listen to the witness of others whose devotion is different from ours. Each of these bears testimony to the 'all-powerful Word' who has leapt down 'from the royal throne ... into the heart of a doomed land' with the message of 'peace on earth'.

Prayer

Lord, when peaceful silence lay over all,

your all powerful Word leapt down into our doomed land, revealed to us in a mother's son, announced to us in angelic messages of peace, goodwill.

Grant us grace to taste and see the sweetness of your gift of your Son, whom Mary bore in unselfish submission to your will, and to respond in obedience and self-giving love, as we wait in hope for his coming again.

---

3   Robert Ellsberg, *Blessed Among Us* (Liturgical Press, p. 682)

Christmas Day
Done for love

Over several years Christmas morning began for me in prison. Early, after the splendour of candlelit Midnight Mass celebrated amongst free, happy people, the contrast could not have been greater. In the grey prison, among the condemned, discriminated against and forgotten of God's children, we shared the Christmas story, sang carols and offered the gifts of bread and wine to all who would receive. In the few brief hours that followed, visiting the different wings, listening to stories, sharing hard-earned Christmas treats, I received some of the most treasured gifts of any Christmas.

One of the prisons I visited was closed down, and I was invited to the closing ceremony. Little was left, the doors were all opened, including to the chamber where once those who had been hanged dropped. A sobering moment. Yet outside I was presented with the last item to leave the prison - an icon of Christ and his mother, drawn for me by one of the former inmates, now dispersed anonymously to another jail.

Gazing at that icon, I noticed what a friend once pointed out, that icons of Mary are marked by very dark rings around her eyes. These, she said, symbolised the 'hell of a weight' that both her vocation as 'Christ bearer' and her constant purification from sin demanded. Many in prison were believers. The 'hell of a weight' so many carried was the burden of their past and wrongdoing, alongside their desire to be 'Christ bearers', and their longing to be set free from the burden of sin.

I always found leaving prison to go home difficult. It was not that I did not look forward to all that our family Christmases meant, but somehow in the starkness of prison cells, and the company of men with little in material terms, there was a simplicity of celebration and community. I always received more than I could give. As I drove home, gradually re-adjusting mentally and spiritually to the celebrations ahead, the words, 'Put the desires of your hearts into order, O human beings', echoed in my soul.

Advent began for us in this book with the testimony of Alfred Delp, 'walking up and down my cell three paces this way, three paces that way, my hands in irons and ahead of me an uncertain future'. In these circumstances, Delp observed, 'I have a new understanding of God's promise of redemption and release.' Perhaps too for us this season we have grasped something of a 'new understanding of redemption and release.'

Delp began his reflection by saying that, 'There is perhaps nothing we modern people need more than to be genuinely shaken up.' Through these weeks of Advent, in the stories, reflections and encounters we have made, we have seen occasions to 'Put the desires of our hearts into order'.

And now it is Christmas Day. Once again Christ *is come*. Come as a newborn baby whom we have a chance to love, giving us an opportunity to give him something through what we give in love to others. I love the story of the little American boy who cleaned his mother's shoes to a bright shine. Proud as punch he presented the boots to his mother, who rewarded him with a 'quarter'.

The next morning, as the mother put on her boots, she felt a lump against her foot. Removing the boot, she found a piece of paper wrapped round a coin. On the paper was written in a child's hand-writing: 'I done it for love'. In his own simple way the boy expressed the true spirit of Christ's coming among us. It is done for love.

This morning the nativity scene is complete. The babe has been wrapped in a piece of torn hanky and laid in the manger. Because at Carol services the whole gamut of stories associated with the 'babe lying in the manger' are read, we have shepherds with their gifts of lambs; and Magi with their gold, frankincense and myrrh, already gathered in the stable. A record of an event that almost certainly did not take place in quite that way. But does that matter? Surely it is the intent of the story to cause us to wonder upon the graciousness of the gift.

The question Christmas raises is to whom do we give gifts, and who gives us gifts, and why? We have no record of the magi's gold and frankincense; and it is unlikely that the myrrh with which Christ's crucified body was anointed before burial had been kept amongst the treasures Mary held. But it might have been. Neither can we reasonably assume the shepherd's gift of lambs remained, if that is not simply poetic licence to give balance to the nativity tableau. Yet not for nothing did Jesus take to himself the title 'Good Shepherd', and who knows whether that did not occur to him as Mary shared the stories of his birth as he grew through childhood?

What we are left with are the intangibles of gifts represented by devotion, humility, the image of God in the other, whether hidden by unctuous piety or a moment of murdering madness; whether in church or chapel, or a prison rescue shop within a yard of hell. My friend Christine Roberts, to whom I have dedicated this book, and who led Advent retreats for my colleagues and me for over ten years, observed: 'Advent is the time of the people who are small in the world, but who see angels and stars'.

Perhaps then our Christmas response can only be silence. The Christmas story actually tells us very little. Much of what we deduce from it is in the things not said. Yet the 'shaking reality' is that it is in silence that we learn the wisdom of reticence. That though Jesus is the 'Word of God', he comes as infant - from the Latin *in-fans* - not speaking. The Magi arrive without having to say anything, and they are allowed to leave without instruction, to discover what they have learned in their own way.

The 'shaking reality' of Christmas is that we are invited to be 'born again', to re-engage with what is authentic, real; so that we may grow in our understanding of 'God's promise of redemption and release'; of compassion, to peace within, that we might be signs of resurrection.

Happy Christmas.

Prayer

Lord, grant to us this Christmas grace
like Mary, to hear the whisper of the angels;
like Joseph, to receive the fragment of a dream;
like the shepherds, to hear a new song;
and like the Magi to catch a glimpse of light.

Appreciation

'We do and we do not want to welcome Advent', observed Chris on one of our annual retreats. Telling a story of a little boy in a care home who was reluctant to attend a party being held for the children, she recalled a question asked by the child's carer, as she sought to persuade him to come: 'Do you need to put your courage skin on?'

The 'shaking reality' of Advent is that in its own way it invites us all to answer the question: 'Do you need to put your courage skin on?' In preparing this book I have been grateful for the help and insights of a number of people who took the trouble to say 'Yes' to my request to reflect on the material in this book. Each of them has contributed something to the final work, sometimes with a question, others with a new insight, others still with suggestions for brevity or clarity.

I am particularly appreciative of former colleagues, Bishop Peter Maurice, Caroline Turner, Christine Treanor, as well as friends, Maureen Bollard, Katy Hayward, Sylvia Roberts, Carol Stickland, for their diligence and care. Daphne Jowit too used it as a resource, but I am particularly grateful to her for her sharp-eyed editing and tidying up of my grammar, sentence structure and ensuring consistency.

My wife Dee persuaded me to make it our Advent reflection in an earlier form. With some reluctance I agreed on the understanding that the gaffes and critique remained unremarked upon until we reached Christmas. Each night we followed our

Advent ritual of which I spoke at the beginning of the book, but with a certain impish sense of humour Dee insisted that as we opened each day's Advent box, there would be a joke. They were universally corny - 'Why does Santa ban smoking?' 'Because it is bad for your elf?' was one such contribution. Yet at the same time they gave perspective to the demands of Advent's 'shaking reality', reminding us that God's love extends to the frivolous as well as total self-giving.

For a number of years between 2002 -2013 leading up to Advent, Christine Roberts led a number of clergy retreats with great wisdom and skill in the diocese of which I was bishop. Without her imagination, wisdom and tenacity the season of Advent would have been marked less reflectively and transformationally through those years. The style and nature of our reflection is different, but the significance of Advent in Christian observation has been enhanced because of those encounters. In some small way I hope this book offers hope to readers, and is a worthy testimony to a remarkable teacher, guide and friend.

My final thanks are to the ongoing trust and confidence of David Moloney, Helen Porter, Will Parkes, and the team at Darton, Longman and Todd, for their willingness to risk this further work from me.

Peter B. Price